This agenda belongs to:

NAME ______________________________

ADDRESS ______________________________

CITY/TOWN ______________________ ZIP CODE __________

PHONE ______________________________

STUDENT NO. ______________________________

PLEASE NOTE: The front cover is sensitive to extreme heat. Do not leave in direct sunlight!

Printed on recyclable paper

CPSIA: Premier Agendas Inc, Bellingham, WA, PY2011-12

STUDENT SERVICES

Paris Junior College offers students a wide variety of special services to make the college experience worthwhile and rewarding. The faculty and staff are personally involved and feel responsibility, along with the students, for student success or failure. This philosophy of accountability places much emphasis on each individual (faculty and student) and challenges them to do their best toward giving students their moral right — the right to have the best education possible.

The best method to take advantage of your educational opportunity is for you to participate in the special services designed and programmed for you. All of these programs and services have been organized to meet your in-class and after-class needs.

» ***Homework assistance, walk-in, individual and small-group tutoring.*** Found at Tutoring (Learning Resource Center #105), Monday-Thursday 8 am-9 pm. Paris campus: 903-782-0270; Greenville Center: 903-454-9333 (call for times); Sulphur Springs Center: 903-885-1232 (call for times).

» ***Degree plans, schedule preparation, career planning, disabilities, international students, and veterans information.*** Found at Counseling & Advising (Alford Center). Paris campus: 903-782-0426; Greenville Center: 903-454-9333; Sulphur Springs Center: 903-885-1232.

» ***Assistance with log-in for distance education classes.*** Found at Distance Education (Learning Resource Center #124). 903-782-0436 or 903-782-0311; khaley@parisjc.edu or dhelliwell@parisjc.edu.

» ***Resources, databases, reference materials, books, and computers.*** Found at the Library (Learning Resource Center). Paris: 903-782-0415; Greenville Center: 903-457-8729; Sulphur Springs Center: 903-439-6154, ext. 410.

» ***Assistance with writing papers.*** Found at the Writing Center (Administration Building #125). Paris campus: 903-782-0314; Monday, Wednesday and Thursday 8:30 am-12 pm and 1-4:30 pm; Tuesday 8am-9pm; Friday 9am-12pm.

» ***Free educational outreach program helping adults pursue training programs.*** Found at the EOC (Bob Berry Complex). Paris campus: 903-782-0353; Greenville Center: 903-454-8706; Sulphur Springs Center: 903-885-1232.

» ***Assistance with math problems.*** Found at the Math Lab/Tutoring (Natural Science #122). Paris campus: 903-782-0209; Monday-Thursday 9am-12pm and 1-4pm; Friday 9am-12pm.

Who do I call for What?

» ***GED Testing, placement assessments, proctoring exams, online testing.*** Call the Testing Center in the Alford Center. Paris campus: 903-782-0446; Greenville Center: 903-454-9333; Sulphur Springs Center: 903-439-6154, ext. 410.

» ***Your PJC e-mail account to stay in touch with the college and instructors at Dragon E-mail.*** Contact 903-782-0489 or redmonson@parisjc.edu.

» ***Purchase materials, supplies and books at the College Store.*** Paris campus: 903-782-0344; Greenville Center: 903-457-8731.

» ***Student ID's and campus safety at Security.*** Call 903-782-0399.

» ***View grades, unofficial transcripts, register online at Campus Connect.*** Call 903-782-0212.

» ***Transcripts, graduation, degree audit at Records (Administration Building #138).*** Call 903-782-0212.

» ***Pell Grant, loans, awards, veterans information at Financial Aid (Alford Center).*** Call 903-782-0429.

» ***Tours, transfer information, registration, general questions at Admissions (Administration***

Building #149). Call 903-782-0425.

» ***Pay bills, FACTS, payment plans at the Business Office (Administration Building #136).*** Call 903-782-0232.

FINANCIAL AID

GENERAL INFORMATION

Paris Junior College subscribes to the philosophy that all students who have the ability to pursue and can benefit from a college education should be given the opportunity. The purpose of federal financial aid is to provide grants and part-time employment to eligible students who need help with paying their college expenses.

Because students are the ones who will benefit the most from their college education, the students and their families are considered to have primary responsibility for paying the costs of attendance. Federal financial aid is only intended to supplement, not replace, the student's and their family's responsibility for paying college expenses.

Paris Campus
For detailed information about the federal financial aid programs and institutional policies and procedures, students are advised to contact the Financial Aid office on the Paris campus.

Greenville and Sulphur Springs Centers
For detailed information about the federal financial aid programs and institutional policies and procedures, students are advised to contact the financial aid advisor during posted hours.

Award Procedures

All federal and state financial aid is awarded in strict compliance with federal and state regulations and institutional policies and procedures. Priority is given to students with the greatest documented financial need whose completed applications are received by the priority dates.

Federal financial aid is awarded on the basis of documented individual need. Need is the difference between the college's estimated cost of attendance for the student and the amount the students and family can reasonably be expected to contribute toward the student's cost of attendance. Need based aid awards cannot exceed documented financial need.

The major need-based federal financial aid programs are the Federal Pell Grant, Federal College Work Study, Federal Supplemental Educational Opportunity Grant programs and the federal direct subsidized and unsubsidized Stafford Loan programs. A grant does not have to be paid back if the recipient complies with all of the terms under which the money was awarded. Work study gives the student the opportunity to work at the college and earn money to help pay expenses. Student loans must be repaid under the terms of the loan.

Perkins Loans and Parent Plus Loans are not an option at this institution.

The State of Texas has many special grant and exemption programs that may be available to eligible Texas residents. See the College For Texans Web site (www.collegefortexans.com) for available programs of interest.

Federal Direct Student Loan Restrictions

In accordance with federal regulations, a school must verify that a loan recipient is meeting SAP each time funds are released to the student. If you have been awarded money under the Direct Loans, all or part of your loan will be canceled if you are not meeting SAP at the time loan funds are available for disbursement (distribution).

You then will not be considered for future loans until the SAP requirements have been met. Other restrictions related to your college's default management plan may limit how much you may borrow and when you will receive your loan payments.

VETERAN'S AFFAIRS AND BENEFITS

Paris Campus
Paris Junior College is approved for veterans training under the provisions of various federal and state laws. Veteran affairs are administered through the Office of Student Financial Aid located in the Alford Center.

Greenville and Sulphur Springs Centers
Contact financial aid advisor during posted hours.

Veterans who are applying for VA educational benefits are advised to call VA to inquire and verify VA eligibility. Telephone number: VA Regional Office, 1-888-442-4551.

SCHOLARSHIPS

Paris Junior College offers an extensive range of scholarship programs. The criteria for selecting scholarship recipients may include, but is not limited to, academic achievement, major area of study, service to the college, leadership and personal character. All recipients of Paris Junior College scholarships are required to complete a Free Application for Federal Student Aid (FAFSA).

Students interested in applying for a specific institutional scholarship should contact the Admissions Office or the Financial Aid Office (Paris Campus) for detailed information.

COUNSELING/ADVISING CENTER

COUNSELING/ADVISING

Counselors and advisors assist students in making plans and decisions concerning their academic careers. Counselors address each individual student's needs for personal and career development. Programs have been developed to assist all students including special populations and non-traditional students. Counselors assist students in selecting careers, in resolving personal problems and in managing stress. Confidential counseling is provided to assist students in coping with academic concerns and in resolving personal situations that may impede academic success. Students may find counseling services helpful as they make plans and decisions in various phases of their academic career. Counselors and advisors help students in the selection of appropriate educational programs, with the selection of courses and with the scheduling of classes. Services provided by the Counseling/Advising Center include personal counseling, career planning, academic advising, disability services, career libraries, computerized guidance, transfer services, academic advising for veterans and international student services. Students may contact a counselor or advisor at the Alford Center, Paris campus, or call 903-782-0426 (Paris campus), 903-454-9333 (Greenville campus) or 903-885-1232 (Sulphur Springs campus) to schedule an appointment with a counselor or advisor.

CAREER PLANNING

Students and alumni are encouraged to utilize the career planning services of the Counseling/Advising Center to assist them in making career decisions. The goal of career services is to promote career development by providing students with the knowledge and skills needed to develop appropriate career plans and help them develop decision making skills to accomplish those career goals. Services include career counseling with a counselor to explore career options through the use of various tests and inventories, computer based career systems, occupational information, transfer and course equivalency information. A comprehensive career library provides students the opportunity to research information about job search strategies, resume writing, career fields, self-help resources and career information. For more information, students may contact a career counselor at the Counseling/Advising Center, Alford Center, Paris campus, or may call 903-782-0426 (Paris campus), 903-454-9333 (Greenville campus) or 903-885-1232 (Sulphur Springs campus) to schedule an appointment with a career counselor.

SERVICES FOR STUDENTS WITH DISABILITIES

Services for students with disabilities are coordinated by the Counseling/Advising Center (Paris campus). Services include arrangements for accommodations, counseling, and services to allow equal access to educational opportunities for students with disabilities. Students must request services by providing a letter of verification of disability and must complete an interview with a Counseling/Advising Center counselor or advisor. Reasonable accommodation request(s) with documentation may be subject to review by the ADA Committee.

To provide appropriate planning and scheduling, students must submit their requests at least two weeks before accommodations are needed. For scheduling of interpreters, available modified equipment, enlarged text and/or books on tape, please allow four to six weeks.

For more information, contact Counseling/Advising at 903-782-0426 (Paris campus). Students are encouraged to seek assistance in advance of the beginning of the semester in which accommodations are requested.

TUTORING

All tutoring is free. Students seeking tutoring services should come to the Rheudasil Learning Center (Paris campus) or contact an advisor at the Greenville or Sulphur Springs campus.

TRANSFER SERVICES

Paris Junior College offers students assistance in the transition to a four-year institution. Students are encouraged to take advantage of the resources available to assist them in making informed decisions regarding course selection, choosing a senior institution, and in successfully completing the transfer process.

The Counseling/Advising Center (Paris campus) houses a large collection of senior institution catalogs, admission application forms, and general information bulletins and brochures. Students can also utilize the SIGI, Discover or Texas CARES computerized guidance systems to aid in researching information on senior institutions and to help in identifying career and occupational interests. Students may also contact a Counseling/Advising Center advisor at the Greenville or Sulphur Springs campuses to obtain transfer information.

College Day, where senior institutions are available to provide information directly to students, transfer workshops, and career seminars are activities that directly assist the Paris Junior College transfer student in making the transition a successful one. For further information contact the Counseling/Advising Center located in the Alford Center (Paris campus).

STUDENT LIFE AND ACTIVITIES

The college encourages many types of programs — cultural, social and athletic — in the hope that the students' interests will be developed as fully as possible. An education at Paris Junior College means more than attending classes.

The needs and desires of students are the basis for the types of activities presented at the college. A wide variety of organizations are available to meet these needs, and give students the opportunity to become involved in planning activities, making new friends, developing leadership qualities, developing individual and group interests, and receiving recognition for accomplishments. Student Activities sponsors events for the entire college community including a variety of competitive sports, dances, speakers, intercollegiate athletics, intramurals, recreational programs, community service projects and leadership opportunities.

Your activity card (I.D. card) furnished at registration is your "admission ticket" to most campus events.

Student Government Association

A student council was formed in 1937. The organization and constitution were reorganized in 1970, and renamed the Student Government Association with the executive officers elected by the student body. Vice presidents of all student organizations automatically are members of the student governing body. The chief duties of the Student Government Association, working with the faculty and administration, are: conducting student elections, arranging the social calendar for the year, providing equitable representation within the student association of each student organization, discussion of campus affairs as they pertain to student life, and planning the course of action for implementation of these activities and programs. This governmental agency provides policy making decisions over all student organizations and serves to promote better relations between the administration and the students and to protect the best interests of the students. The Student Government Association holds membership in the Texas Junior College Government Association.

Intramurals

The intramural sports program provides structured, competitive and non-competitive sport opportunities for men, women and co-intramural participants. The program offers a variety of tournaments for students, faculty and staff. The program does not require the intensified training and high degree of skill associated with varsity athletes. An individual's playing ability is not considered as important as his/her desire to enter into the true spirit of competition and good sportsmanship. A few of the sports organized for Paris Junior College students, faculty and staff are basketball, volleyball, and flag football. Information concerning these sports and others, may be obtained from the Student Activities Coordinator in the Student Center, room 215.

Informal Sports

Paris Campus

The informal sports program involves a process of self-directed participation. It is an individualized approach to sport which allows students to participate for fun and fitness. A current PJC I.D. card is required for admission to the Old Gymnasium and Weight and Fitness Center, during informal sports hours, Sunday through Thursday, 5 p.m. to 9 p.m.

College Calendar

The official College Calendar is located in the Division of Student Life (Paris campus). Students are encouraged to consult the Director of Student Life prior to planning their programs and events. Generally, with the exception of student organizational meetings, activity events are not permitted to conflict.

STUDENT ORGANIZATIONS

Various clubs and societies have been organized to meet the extra-curricular needs of Paris Junior College students. These organizations give students the opportunity to become involved in planning activities, developing leadership qualities, developing individual interests, and receiving recognition for accomplishments.

Student activity organizations are open to all students. However, certain curriculum-oriented clubs may limit their membership to students enrolled in that curriculum, and other clubs may require a member to maintain a certain scholastic average.

Students are encouraged to initiate and develop organizations consistent with the purposes and philosophy of Paris

Junior College. The procedures for organizing a new club may be obtained from the Student Life Office in the J.R. McLemore Student Center.

Phi Theta Kappa

Phi Theta Kappa is the only national scholastic honor society for junior colleges recognized by the American Association of Community Colleges. It was founded in 1918, and a local chapter has been at PJC since 1932. Its purpose is the promotion of scholarship, development of leadership and service, and cultivation of fellowship among students.

To be eligible for membership, a student must have completed one long-term semester at Paris Junior College, must have accumulated 12 semester hours (exclusive of developmental courses), have a grade point average of 3.5, and be within the upper scholastic 10 percent of the regularly enrolled student body.

To maintain active membership, a student must be regularly enrolled each semester, and at the end of any given semester must have a grade point average of 3.0, which is a "B".

Phi Theta Kappa is an active organization on all campuses, Paris, Greenville, and Sulphur Springs.

Religious Organizations

Paris Campus
Baptist Student Ministry — The Baptist Student ministry (BSM) is comprised of Baptist students as well as other students who are interested in participating in the club's activities. The organization meets each Monday, Tuesday and Thursday in the Religious Activities Center. Consult your calendar for times.

United Campus Ministry — The United Campus Ministry of Paris Junior College is an organization of students interested in exploring the meaning of the Christian faith through study, discussion and service. In the past, the group has engaged in tutoring programs for elementary students, recreation for children at Booker T. Washington Homes, and voter registration. Regular meetings are every Tuesday, Wednesday and Thursday at 11:30 am, with a free meal provided by member churches.

Special Populations

The Connect Program, designed for special populations, provides textbook loans and childcare funding assistance to qualified students. To be considered for this program, a student must have a declared workforce education major. Special population categories include the following:

- Student with a disability;
- Student training for a non-traditional major for their gender;
- Student who is economically disadvantaged.
- Student with limited English proficiency.

This program offers personal and career counseling, and referral services for participants. Also, students are encouraged to take advantage of job preparation services such as resume writing and job interviewing materials.

To obtain an application for the Connect Program, students may go to room 103 of the Alford Building on the Paris campus or call 903.782.0426. Greenville students may go to the Main Office or call 903.454.9333, and Sulphur Springs students may go to the Main Office or call 903.885.1232.

Support Groups

Other students provide a support network to help with the educational, emotional, interpersonal and family demands of returning to school.

Workshops

You can become self-sufficient by learning how to manage stress, money, time, personal choices, career plans, childcare and health. Students must attend at least two Special Populations workshops a semester. Workshop dates will be announced and/or posted throughout the semester.

Referrals

The Special Populations Coordinator can help you get in contact with other community social services and educational departments if you need additional assistance.

For more information about the services for single parents, single pregnant women, displaced homemakers, and students enrolled in a non-traditional field, contact the Special Populations office in the Applied Sciences building (Paris campus).

Special Populations services are available on all campuses.

ACADEMIC POLICIES

Advising

All new PJC (first-time and transfer) students will meet with an academic advisor and prepare a degree plan. PJC students will be notified regarding designated academic advising times prior to early registration for the fall and spring semester. Registration dates will be published in the schedule of classes.

During the registration process, all students meet with an advisor to select courses and update, or complete degree plans. Students whose local placement or THEA scores indicate a need for remediation must first be advised by a member of the developmental education staff. Students are then directed to the appropriate area to meet with a faculty member from their major discipline to receive guidance in selecting courses. Students who have not selected an area of study meet with a member of the student development staff or designated faculty member to clarify goals and achieve advice about scheduling classes. Upon completion of the schedule, both the student and the advisor sign the advising/enrollment form, documenting the process of advising.

Advising Materials

Critical information must be available for the Paris Junior College staff to be able to give you good advice. You should bring this information with you to registration. If possible, you should provide:

» High school transcript
» Transcripts of work transferred to Paris Junior College
» Local assessment test scores (it is best to complete local assessment prior to registration)
» ACT or SAT scores, if available
» THEA if available
» Record of Paris Junior College work completed
» Degree plan (completed and updated by an advisor)
» Catalog from the college to which you intend to transfer

Satisfactory Progress

Students are required to be making satisfactory academic progress at the time they receive federal and state financial aid. Students receiving these funds at Paris Junior College will be considered to be achieving satisfactory academic progress as long as both of the following conditions are met:

» If paid as a full-time student (12 hours or more); must successfully complete at least 9 credit hours; if paid as a part-time student (3/4, 1/2, <1/2); must successfully complete all hours for which they are paid.*

› * Successfully complete, means an A, B, C, D or X grade.

» Complete these courses with a minimum cumulative grade point average of 2.0.

Generally students may receive financial assistance during their first 90 semester hours of course work taken at Paris Junior College, whether or not financial aid was previously received.

STUDENT POLICIES

ACADEMIC ACHIEVEMENT CREDIT (EGA)

Grading System

Paris Junior College is on a four point grading system. Grades and grade points for each semester hour of credit are as follows:

» A - Excellent: 4 grade points per credit hour
» B - Above Average: 3 grade points per credit hour
» C - Average: 2 grade points per credit hour
» D - Below Average: 1 grade point per credit hour
» F - Failure: 0 grade points per credit hour
» W - Withdrawal: 0 grade points per credit hour
» X- Incomplete: 0 grade points per credit hour

Grades of "W" and "X" are not included in the computation of cumulative grade point averages. A grade of "W" indicates that the student withdrew from class. A grade of "X" indicates that course work was incomplete at the end of the semester.

The instructor must submit a Request for Change of Grade to the Records Office when all course work has been completed. Incomplete course work must be completed by the end of the next long semester, or the grade of "X" shall be changed to a grade of "F".

Raising a Grade

A grade in a course may be raised only by the student's repeating the course and making a higher grade.

Grade Reports

Paris Junior College does not mail grade reports. For grade reports, use Campus Connect from the PJC system or from any computer connected to the Internet.

Student Classification

A student is classified as a freshman with credit for fewer than 30 semester hours. A student is classified as a sophomore with credit for 30 or more semester hours.

Academic Probation and Suspension

Students must maintain a cumulative grade point average of at least 2.0 for all course work attempted during the fall and/or spring semesters. Special program students and scholarship students may require higher grade point average status to continue. The student should be familiar with the regulations dealing with scholastic probation and enforced withdrawal. These standards are published in the PJC student handbook, procedures manual and the policy manual.

In addition, students are advised about the probation and suspension policies during the required freshman learning frameworks course. A student who has been dismissed, but who nevertheless registers in the College, shall have his/

her registration cancelled and cannot attend classes. Such a student will receive no special consideration on a plea of lack of knowledge of his scholastic status, regardless of whether he registered and paid his fees.

Students shall maintain a cumulative grade point average of at least 2.0 on all course work attempted during the fall and/or spring semesters.

Probation

Students who have a cumulative grade point average of less than 2.0 for all course work attempted during the fall or spring semesters shall be placed on academic probation. Students may remove all probation status by raising their cumulative grade point average to a 2.0 or higher during the fall, spring, or summer semesters.

Strict Probation

Students who remain on academic probation for two consecutive semesters shall be placed on strict probation for the subsequent semester. Students on strict probation must achieve a cumulative grade point average of at least 2.0 by the end of the semester. Failure to achieve the required cumulative grade point average shall result in suspension from the institution for one long term (fall or spring).

Suspension

Students who fail to remove academic deficiencies while on strict probation shall be suspended from the institution. Under certain circumstances students on suspension may be readmitted by the institution on strict probation. Students who have been suspended from the institution two times shall normally be denied future admission to the institution.

Strict Probation Admission

A student who is on suspension from the College or another accredited institution may request admission to the College on strict probation. The request must be made in person to the Director of Admissions. If, in the opinion of the Director of Admissions, the student has the ability to continue pursuing college work, the student may be readmitted on strict probation.

Students on probation and strict probation shall meet all of the following requirements:

» Contact an advisor from the Counseling/Advising Center prior to registration to seek approval for your schedule.

» Enroll for no more than 12 credit hours.

» Meet with an advisor from the Counseling/Advising Center at least twice during the semester to provide an academic report concerning progress in course(s).

Students readmitted on strict probation shall meet all of the following requirements:

» Prior to registration, you must contact a counselor/advisor from the Counseling/Advising Center to have your schedule approved.

» You may not register online.

» You may not enroll for more than 12 credit hours, excluding one hour kinesiology courses and one hour learning skills courses.

» You must enroll for a study skills and/or Learning Frameworks course.

» You will be required to meet monthly with your advisor during the semester to provide an academic report concerning your progress, as well as work closely with your instructors.

» Contact each instructor on a regular basis for special instructions and assistance, as needed.

» You will forfeit eligibility for any student activity, club or campus leadership position.

» You will be required to sign a contract indicating your agreement to these terms of Strict Probation.

◊ Paris Junior College wants to make every effort to help you succeed and has established special procedures to help accomplish that goal. You will be asked to follow these procedures and to seek services available to you. Our goal is to help you raise your cumulative grade point average to 2.0 or higher which will remove the probation status.

Student may be administratively withdrawn from all classes by the appropriate vice president for failure to abide by these terms of probation.

Appeal

Decisions concerning academic probation and suspension may be appealed as outlined in FLD (LOCAL).

Student Class Attendance

Students are expected to attend classes on a regular and punctual basis. Absences are considered unauthorized unless the absences are due to sickness, emergencies, or sanctioned school activities. Student's mastery of course content is measured by the individual instructor's criteria. Students may be dropped from classes upon the recommendation of the instructors who believe the students have been unjustifiably absent or tardy a sufficient number of times to preclude meeting the course objectives. Students dropped from classes will receive a grade of "W".

Each instructor must have on file in the respective Dean's office attendance policies, course objectives, and other relevant materials which comprehensively describe the course procedures applicable to each class section. Instructors are responsible for making all students enrolled in their classes aware of these procedures.

When it becomes necessary to drop a student from a class, the instructor will submit a properly completed withdrawal notice to the appropriate Dean. Instructor withdrawals of students may be appealed by the student pursuant to the college's Academic Appeals procedures.

STUDENT'S STANDARD OF CONDUCT (FLB)

Definitions to be used in this policy shall be as follows:

- "Director of Student Life" shall mean an administrator bearing that title, or the officer or officers directly responsible for student programming in the college.
- A "student" shall mean one who is currently enrolled in the college. These policies and regulations shall also apply to any prospective or former students who have been accepted for admission or readmission to any component institution while he or she is on the campus of any component institution.
- The "campus" of the college is defined as all real property over which the college has possession and control.

All students shall obey the law, show respect for properly constituted authority, and observe correct standards of conduct. In addition to activities prohibited by law, the following types of behavior shall be prohibited:

- Gambling, dishonesty, or the excessive use of intoxicating beverages.
- The illegal use, possession and/or sale of a drug or narcotic, as those terms are defined by the Texas Controlled Substances Act.
- Scholastic dishonesty shall constitute a violation of these rules and regulations and is punishable as prescribed by Board policies. Scholastic dishonesty shall include, but not be limited to, cheating on a test, plagiarism and collusion.
  - "Cheating on a test" shall include:
    - Copying from another student's test paper.
    - Using test materials not authorized by the person administering the test.
    - Collaborating with, or seeking aid from, another student during a test without permission from the test administrator.
    - Knowingly using, buying, selling, stealing, or soliciting, in whole or in part, the contents of an unadministered test.

- ◊ The unauthorized transporting or removal, in whole or in part, of the contents of the unadministered test.
- ◊ Substituting for another student, or permitting another student to substitute for one's self, in taking a test.
- ◊ Bribing another person to obtain an unadministered test or information about an unadministered test.

› "Plagiarism" shall be defined as appropriating, buying, receiving, as a gift, or obtaining by any means another's work and the unacknowledged submission or incorporation of it in one's own written work.

› "Collusion" shall be defined as the unauthorized collaboration with another person in preparing written work for fulfillment of course requirements.

- » A student who owes a debt to the college or who writes an "insufficient funds" check to the college may be denied admission or readmission to the college until the debt is paid or the check redeemed.
- » Violations of the Penal Statutes of Texas or of the United States, occurring on college property or in connection with college-sponsored activities, may also constitute violations of the college's rules and regulations when such violations affect the educational process and goals of the college.
- » Possession or use of firearms on college-controlled property, except for educational purposes that have the prior approval of the Director of Student Life (Paris campus).
- » Interference with teaching, research, administration or the college's subsidiary responsibilities through "disorderly conduct" or "disruptive behavior."
- » Use of alcoholic or intoxicating beverages and use of drugs not prescribed by a physician.
- » Hazing, with or without the consent of a student; a violation of that prohibition renders both the person inflicting the hazing and the person submitting to the hazing subject to appropriate discipline.
- » Initiations by organizations may include no feature that is dangerous, harmful or degrading to the student and violation of the prohibition renders the organization subject to appropriate discipline.
- » Endangering the health or safety of members of the college community or visitors to the campus.
- » Damaging or destroying college property.

Any student violating this policy shall be subject to discipline, including suspension.

Dress and Grooming (FLBA)

Students' dress and grooming may not materially and substantially interfere with normal school operations.

Hazing (FLBC)

The college prohibits hazing. "Hazing" means any intentional, knowing or reckless act on or off campus directed against a student, by one person alone or acting with others, that endangers the mental or physical health or safety of a student for the purpose of being initiated into, affiliating with, holding office in, or maintaining membership in any organization whose members are including other students. The term includes, but is not limited to:

- » Any type of physical brutality, such as whipping, beating, striking, branding, electronic shocking, placing of a harmful substance on the body, or similar activity.
- » Any type of physical activity, such as sleep deprivation, exposure to the elements, confinement in a small space, calisthenics, or other activity that subjects the student to an unreasonable risk of harm or that adversely affects the mental or physical health or safety of the student.
- » Any activity involving consumption of a food, liquid, alcoholic beverage, liquor, drug or other substance that subjects the student to an unreasonable risk of harm or that adversely affects the mental or physical health or safety of the student.

- Any activity that intimidates or threatens the student with ostracism, that subjects the student to extreme mental stress, shame, or humiliation, or that adversely affects the mental health or dignity of the student or discourages the student from remaining registered in an educational institution, or that may reasonably be expected to cause a student to leave the organization or the institution rather than submit to acts described above.
- Any activity that induces, causes, or requires the student to perform a duty or task that involves a violation of the Penal Code.

The following actions shall be included in the offense of hazing; students who commit any of them violate college policy and are also subject to criminal prosecution:

- Engaging in hazing.
- Soliciting, encouraging, directing, aiding, attempting to aid another in engaging in hazing.
- Intentionally, knowingly or recklessly permitting hazing to occur.
- Having firsthand knowledge of the planning of a specific hazing incident involving a student, or firsthand knowledge that a specific hazing incident has occurred, and knowingly failing to report that knowledge in writing to the Director of Student Life (Paris campus).

Cellular Phones, Beepers and Personal Digital Assistants (pda's)

All cell phones, beepers and personal digital assistants (pda's) must be turned off or in silent mode. Under no circumstances should a cell phone or beeper sound during class. If a cell phone or beeper does sound during class the student my be asked to leave for the remainder of the period. The only exception to this rule includes peace officers, EMT, EMS, or other emergency personnel, and their devices should be in silent mode.

Smoking

The use of tobacco and tobacco-related products, including smokeless tobacco, is prohibited in all indoor public areas of the campus. Smoking shall not be allowed within 25 feet of doors to public buildings. Smoking kiosks are available for students and employees who smoke. Smoking and tobacco-related products are not permitted inside Hub Hollis baseball field complex.

Alcohol and Drug Use (FLBE)

The use of intoxicating beverages shall be prohibited in classroom buildings, student housing, laboratories, auditoriums, library buildings, museums, faculty and administrative offices, intercollegiate and intramural athletic facilities, and all other public campus areas; however, with prior consent of the Board, the provisions herein may be waived with respect to any specific affair that is sponsored by the institution. State law shall be strictly enforced at all times on all property controlled by the college in regard to the possession and consumption of alcoholic beverages.

No student shall possess, use, transmit or attempt to possess, use or transmit or be under the influence of (legal intoxication not required) any of the following substances on school premises during any school term or off-school premises at a school-sponsored activity, function or event:

- Any controlled substance or dangerous drug as defined by law, including but not limited to marijuana, any narcotic drug, hallucinogen, stimulant, depressant, amphetamine or barbiturate.
- Alcohol or any alcoholic beverage.
- Any abusable glue, aerosol paint or any other volatile chemical substance for inhalation.
- Any other intoxicant, or mood-changing, mind-altering or behavior-altering drug.

The transmittal, sale or attempted sale of what is represented to be any of the above-listed substances is also prohibited under this policy.

A student who uses a drug authorized by a licensed physician through a prescription, specifically for that student's use, shall not be considered to have violated this rule.

Students who violate this policy shall be subject to appropriate disciplinary action.

Weapons (FLBF)

A student shall not knowingly, intentionally or recklessly go onto the school premises with a firearm, explosive weapon or illegal knife unless pursuant to written regulations or written authorization of the institution. The student shall not interfere with normal activities, occupancy or use of any building or portion of the campus by exhibiting, using or threatening to exhibit or use a firearm.

In addition to the prohibition on firearms, explosive weapons, and illegal knives, students are prohibited from bringing any other weapons on campus or to a college-sponsored activity.

This prohibition shall not normally apply to school supplies such as pencils, compasses and the like, unless those instruments are used in a menacing or threatening manner.

Weapons shall include, but are not limited to the following: (1)fire-arms, (2) fireworks of any kind, (3) clubs, (4) razors, (5) martial arts throwing stars, (6) BB and pellet guns, (7) paint ball guns and (8) potato gun/cannon. All weapons confiscated will not be returned.

Lockers and parked cars on the college premises may be inspected by school personnel if there is reasonable cause to believe they contain weapons.

Students found to be in violation of this policy shall be subject to appropriate disciplinary action, including suspension.

Assaults (FLBG)

Students are prohibited from assaulting any person on college property or while under the college's jurisdiction. An "assault" is defined as:

- » Intentionally, knowingly or recklessly causing bodily injury to another;
- » Intentionally or knowingly threatening another with immediate bodily injury; or
- » Intentionally or knowingly causing physical contact with another when the student knows, or should reasonably believe, that the other will regard the contact as offensive or provocative.

Disruptions (FLBH)

Conduct by students either in or out of class which for any reason — whether because of time, place or manner of behavior — materially disrupts class work or involves substantial disorder or invasion of the rights of others is prohibited.

Student demonstrations and similar activities shall be prohibited when there is evidence that may reasonably lead school authorities to forecast substantial disruption of, or material inference with, normal school operations or approved school activities.

The evidence must support a "reasonable forecast of substantial disruption" of school operations: "undifferentiated fear" or mere apprehension of disturbance is not cause to justify restriction on students, otherwise legitimate right to freedom of expression.

Students who participate in any prohibited activities described above are subject to disciplinary action, based on the severity of the violation and its overall effect on the welfare of other students.

Disorderly conduct shall include any of the following activities occurring on property owned or controlled by the college or at college-sponsored functions.

- » Behavior of a boisterous and tumultuous character such that there is clear and present danger of alarming persons where no legitimate reason for alarm exists.
- » Interference with the peaceful and lawful conduct of persons under circumstances in which there is reason to believe that such conduct will cause or provoke a disturbance.
- » Violent and forceful behavior at any time, such that there is a clear and present danger that free movement of other persons will be impaired.
- » Behavior involving personal abuse or assault when such behavior creates a clear and present danger of causing assaults or fights.
- » Violent, abusive, indecent, profane, boisterous, unreasonably loud or otherwise disorderly conduct under circumstances in which there is reason to believe that such conduct will cause or provoke a disturbance.
- » Willful and malicious behavior that interrupts the speaker of any lawful assembly or impairs the lawful rights of others to participate effectively in such assembly or meeting when there is reason to believe that such conduct will cause or provoke a disturbance.
- » Willful and malicious behavior that obstructs or causes obstruction of any doorway, hall or any other passageway in the college to such an extent that the employees, officers and other persons, including visitors having business with the college, are denied entrance into, exit from, or free passage into such a building.
- » Students are prohibited from bringing infants and small children into the classroom during class sessions or allowing unsupervised children to remain on campus.

Student's Rights and Responsibilities, Interrogations and Searches (FLC)

The college respects the rights of students to privacy and security against arbitrary invasion of their person or property. However, school officials have a limited right to search students or their property when in the interest of the overall welfare of other students, or when necessary to preserve the good order and discipline of the school. If no search warrant is obtained:

- » Any prohibited item within "plain view" is subject to seizure.
- » Residence hall rooms may be searched if probable cause exists and only if exigent circumstances justify not obtaining a search warrant.
  - › Student Life personnel must be in attendance during these searches.

Areas such as lockers and desks, which are owned and controlled by the college, may be searched by school officials when they have reasonable cause to believe that stolen items or items prohibited by law or by Board policy are contained in the area to be searched. Indiscriminate searches in the nature of "fishing expeditions" shall be prohibited. Stolen items and items which are forbidden by Board policy or law may be impounded and may be used as evidence in internal school disciplinary proceedings against the student.

In the event that college law enforcement authorities are involved in a search, Student Life personnel must be in attendance. School searches conducted with the assistance from law enforcement authorities are governed by the Fourth Amendment standards that are applicable in the criminal law context.

Freedom from Discrimination, Harassment, and Retaliation (FDE)

The College District prohibits discrimination, including harassment, against any student on the basis of race, color, religion, gender, national origin, disability, or any other basis prohibited by law. Retaliation against anyone involved in the complaint process is a violation of College district policy.

Discrimination against a student is defined as conduct directed at a student on the basis of race, color, religion, gender, national origin, disability, or on any other basis prohibited by law, that adversely affects the student.

Prohibited harassment of a student is defined as physical, verbal, or nonverbal conduct based on the student's race, color, religion, gender, national origin, disability, or any other basis prohibited by law that is so severe, persistent, or pervasive that the conduct:

- Affects a student's ability to participate in or benefit from an educational program or activity, or creates an intimidating, threatening, hostile, or offensive educational environment;
- Has the purpose or effect of substantially or unreasonably interfering with the student's academic performance; or
- Otherwise adversely affects the student's educational opportunities.

Examples of prohibited harassment may include offensive or derogatory language directed at another person's religious beliefs or practices, accent, skin color, or need for accommodation; threatening or intimidating conduct; offensive jokes, name calling, slurs, or rumors; physical aggression or assault; display of graffiti or printed material promoting racial, ethnic, or other negative stereotypes; or other kinds of aggressive conduct such as theft or damage to property.

Sexual harassment of a student by a College District employee includes unwelcome sexual advances; requests for sexual favors; sexually motivated physical, verbal, or nonverbal conduct; or other conduct or communication of a sexual nature when:

- A College District employe causes the student to believe that the student must submit to the conduct in order to participate in a school program or activity, or that the employee will make an educational decision based on whether or not the student submits to the conduct; or
- The conduct is so severe, persistent, or pervasive that it:
  - Affects the student's ability to participate in or benefit from an educational program or activity, or otherwise adversely affects the student's educational opportunities; or
  - Creates an intimidating, threatening, hostile, or abusive educational environment.

Sexual harassment of a student, including harassment committed by another student, includes unwelcome sexual advances; requests for sexual favors; or sexually motivated physical, verbal, or nonverbal conduct when the conduct is so severe, persistent, or pervasive that it:

- Affects a student's ability to participate in or benefit from an educational program or activity, or creates an intimidating, threatening, hostile, or offensive educational environment;
- Has the purpose or effect of substantially or unreasonably interfering with the student's academic performance; or
- Otherwise adversely affects the student's educational opportunities.

Examples of sexual harassment of a student may include sexual advances; touching intimate body parts or coercing physical contact that is sexual in nature; jokes or conversations of a sexual nature; and other sexually motivated conduct, communications, or contact.

Physical contact not reasonably construed as sexual in nature is not sexual harassment.

The College District prohibits retaliation against a student alleged to have experienced discrimination or harassment or another student who, in good faith, makes a report, serves as a witness, or otherwise participates in an investigation.

A student who intentionally makes a false claim, offers false statements, or refuses to cooperate with a College District investigation regarding discrimination or harassment is subject to appropriate discipline.

Examples of retaliation include threats, unjustified punishments, or unwarranted grade reductions. Unlawful retaliation does not include petty slights or annoyances, such as negative comments that are justified by a student's performance in the classroom.

In this policy, the term "prohibited conduct" includes discrimination, harassment, and retaliation as defined by this policy, even if the behavior does not rise to the level of unlawful conduct.

Any student who believes that he or she has experienced prohibited conduct or believes that another student has experienced prohibited conduct should immediately report the alleged acts to an instructor, counselor, administrator, or other College District employee.

Alternatively, a student may report prohibited conduct directly to one of the College District officials below:
Barbara Thomas, Director of Counseling, 903-782-0426
Kenneth Webb, Director of Student Life, 903-782-0402

Disrespect for Authority

Failure to comply with instructions and directions of college officials and/or law enforcement officers acting in the performance of their duties; or any student who fails to heed a summons to report to an administrative official or instructor's office will not be condoned and subjects himself/herself to immediate disciplinary action from the college.

DRAGON ALERT

In the event of an emergency or severe weather, you can receive an alert sent by text message or e-mail. This is a free service provided by Paris Junior College, though normal message fees may apply. To receive text messages to your cell phone, your cell phone must have text messaging capabilities. Notifications are dependent upon external providers and Paris Junior College cannot guarantee notifications will be received by the intended recipient. To sign up, go to www.parisjc.edu, select the "Current Student" tab at the top of the page, then click the first link under "Important Information Links" and fill out the form and submit it.

http://www.careeronestop.org

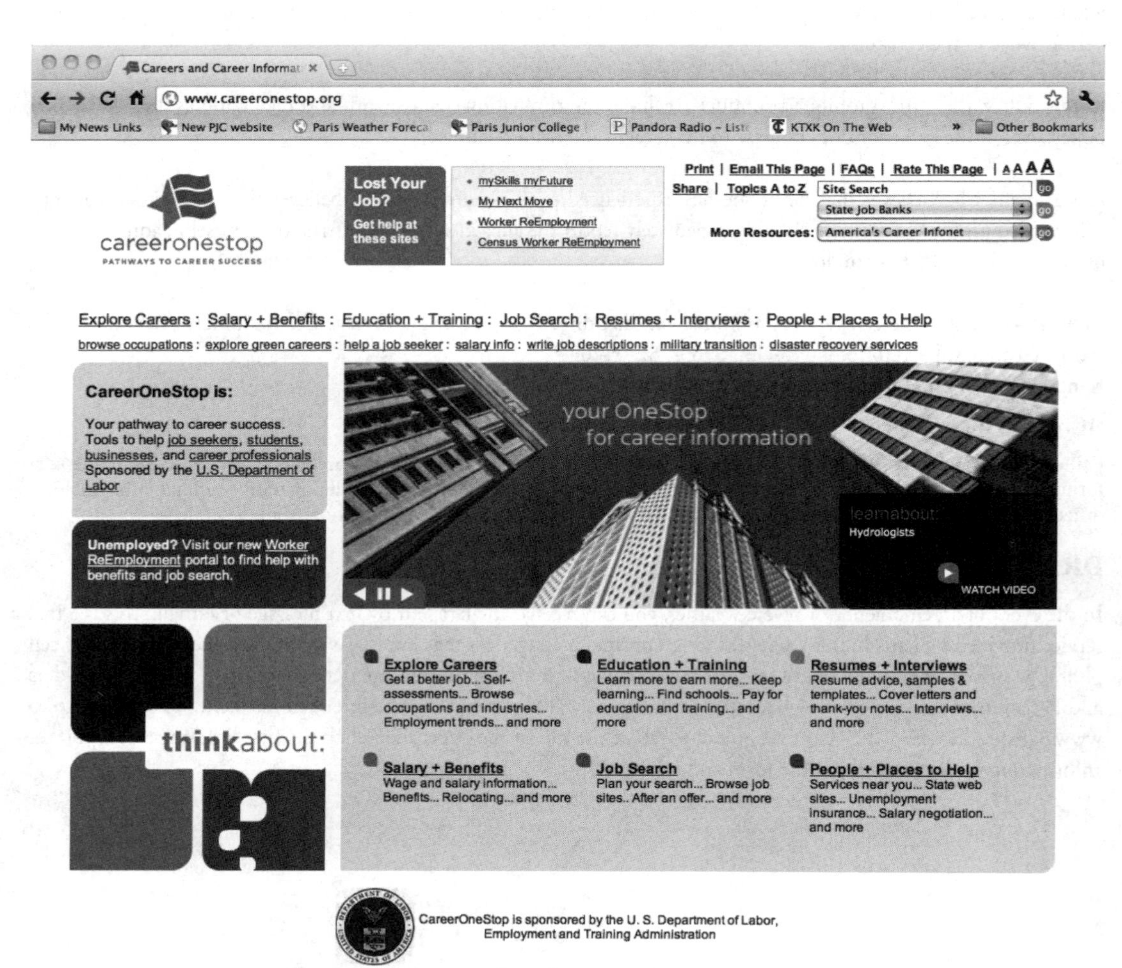

http://www.careeronestop.org

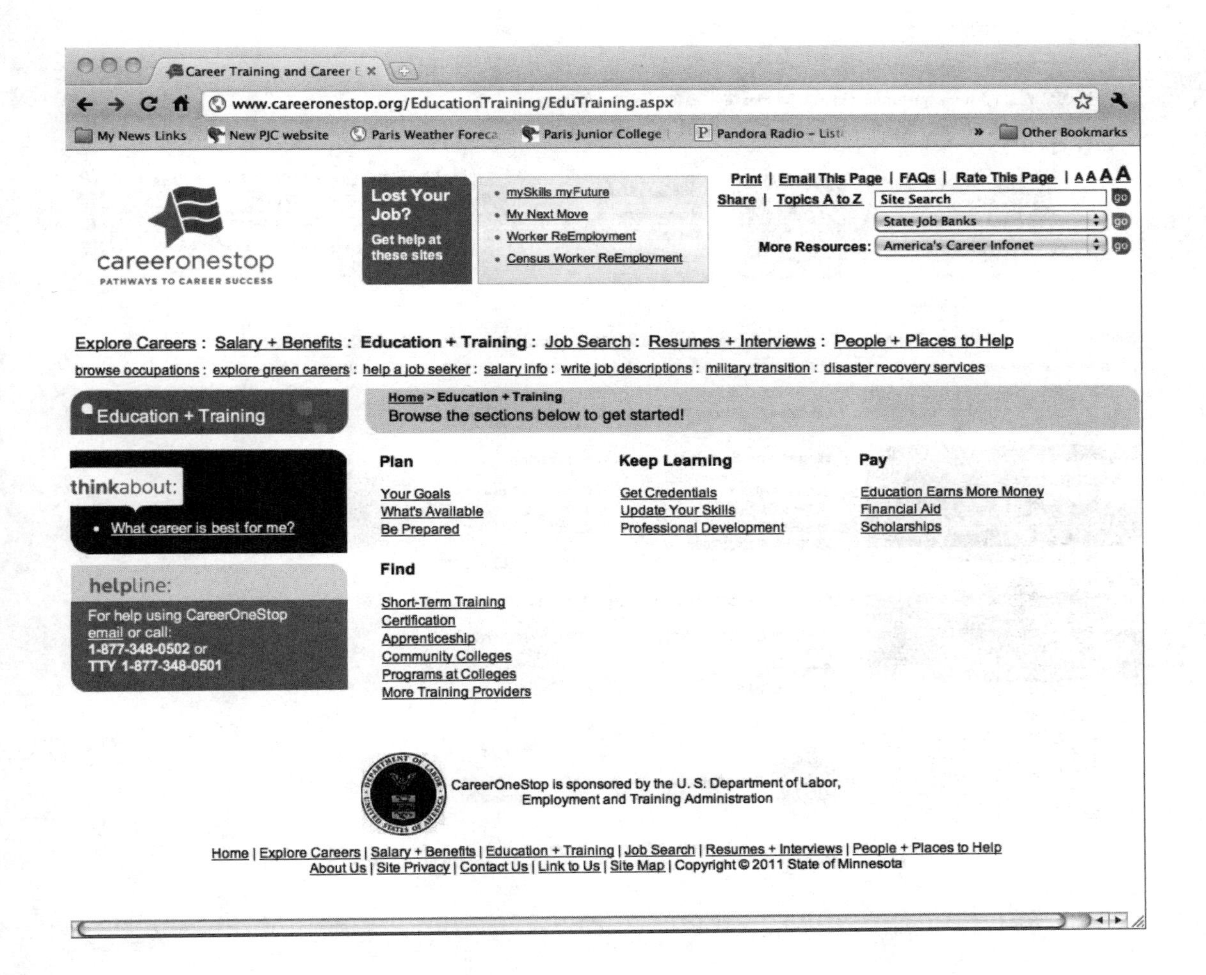

http://www.careeronestop.org

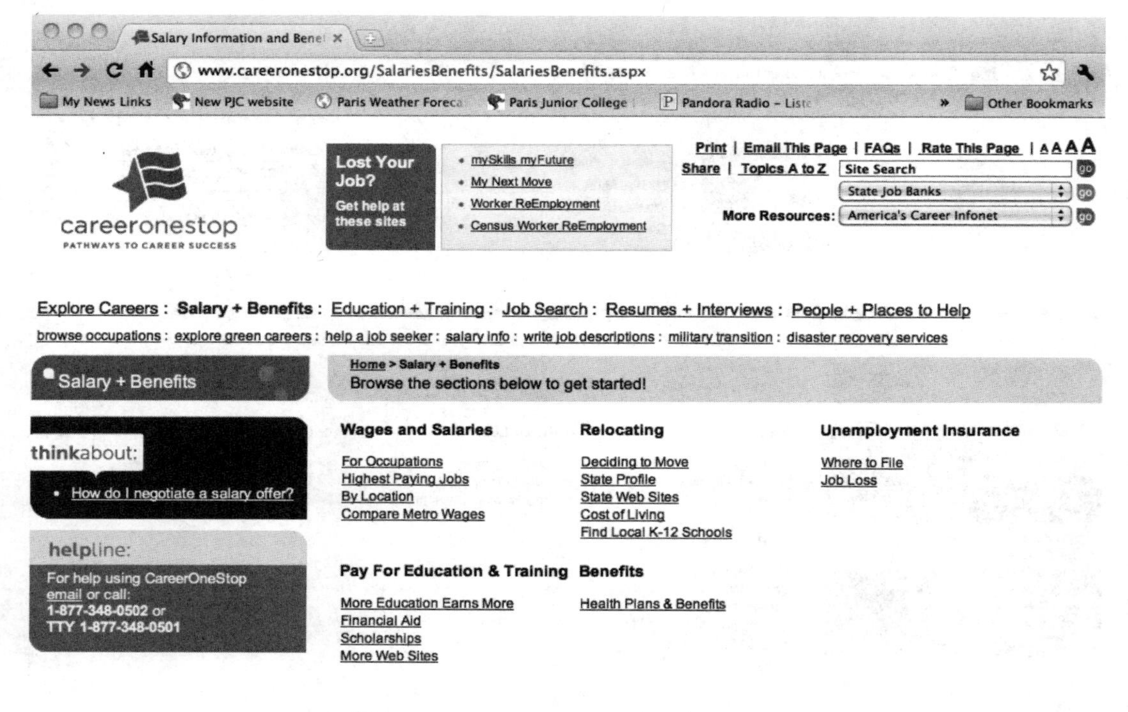

http://www.careeronestop.org

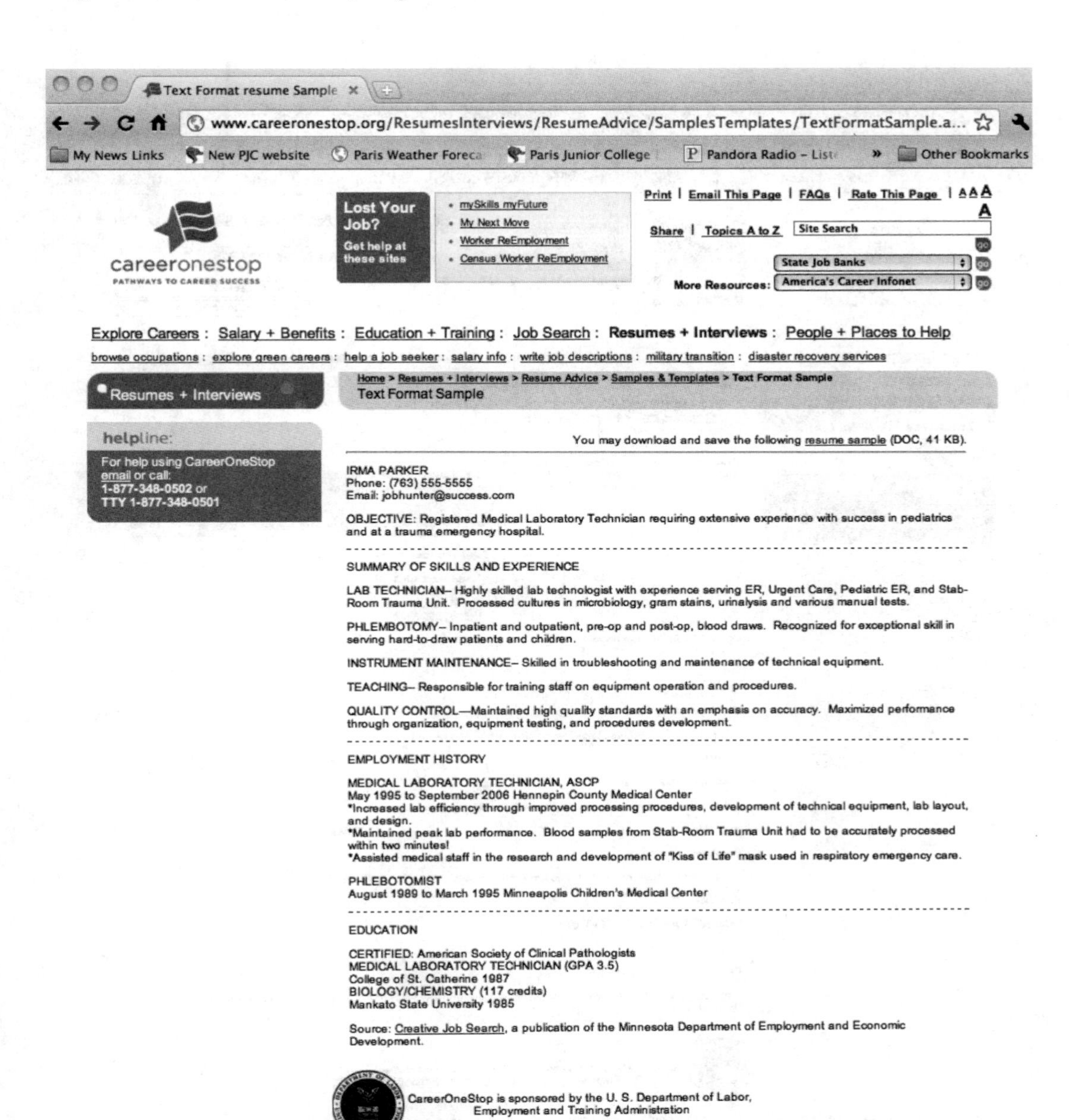

Text Format resume Sample

www.careeronestop.org/ResumesInterviews/ResumeAdvice/SamplesTemplates/TextFormatSample.a...

My News Links | New PJC website | Paris Weather Foreca | Paris Junior College | Pandora Radio - List | » | Other Bookmarks

careeronestop
PATHWAYS TO CAREER SUCCESS

Lost Your Job? Get help at these sites
- mySkills myFuture
- My Next Move
- Worker ReEmployment
- Census Worker ReEmployment

Print | Email This Page | FAQs | Rate This Page | A A A A

Share | Topics A to Z | Site Search

State Job Banks

More Resources: America's Career Infonet

Explore Careers : Salary + Benefits : Education + Training : Job Search : **Resumes + Interviews** : People + Places to Help

browse occupations : explore green careers : help a job seeker : salary info : write job descriptions : military transition : disaster recovery services

Resumes + Interviews

Home > Resumes + Interviews > Resume Advice > Samples & Templates > **Text Format Sample**

Text Format Sample

helpline:
For help using CareerOneStop email or call:
1-877-348-0502 or
TTY 1-877-348-0501

You may download and save the following resume sample (DOC, 41 KB).

IRMA PARKER
Phone: (763) 555-5555
Email: jobhunter@success.com

OBJECTIVE: Registered Medical Laboratory Technician requiring extensive experience with success in pediatrics and at a trauma emergency hospital.

SUMMARY OF SKILLS AND EXPERIENCE

LAB TECHNICIAN– Highly skilled lab technologist with experience serving ER, Urgent Care, Pediatric ER, and Stab-Room Trauma Unit. Processed cultures in microbiology, gram stains, urinalysis and various manual tests.

PHLEMBOTOMY– Inpatient and outpatient, pre-op and post-op, blood draws. Recognized for exceptional skill in serving hard-to-draw patients and children.

INSTRUMENT MAINTENANCE– Skilled in troubleshooting and maintenance of technical equipment.

TEACHING– Responsible for training staff on equipment operation and procedures.

QUALITY CONTROL—Maintained high quality standards with an emphasis on accuracy. Maximized performance through organization, equipment testing, and procedures development.

EMPLOYMENT HISTORY

MEDICAL LABORATORY TECHNICIAN, ASCP
May 1995 to September 2006 Hennepin County Medical Center
*Increased lab efficiency through improved processing procedures, development of technical equipment, lab layout, and design.
*Maintained peak lab performance. Blood samples from Stab-Room Trauma Unit had to be accurately processed within two minutes!
*Assisted medical staff in the research and development of "Kiss of Life" mask used in respiratory emergency care.

PHLEBOTOMIST
August 1989 to March 1995 Minneapolis Children's Medical Center

----

EDUCATION

CERTIFIED: American Society of Clinical Pathologists
MEDICAL LABORATORY TECHNICIAN (GPA 3.5)
College of St. Catherine 1987
BIOLOGY/CHEMISTRY (117 credits)
Mankato State University 1985

Source: Creative Job Search, a publication of the Minnesota Department of Employment and Economic Development.

CareerOneStop is sponsored by the U. S. Department of Labor, Employment and Training Administration

Home | Explore Careers | Salary + Benefits | Education + Training | Job Search | Resumes + Interviews | People + Places to Help
About Us | Site Privacy | Contact Us | Link to Us | Site Map | Copyright © 2011 State of Minnesota

http://www.careeronestop.org

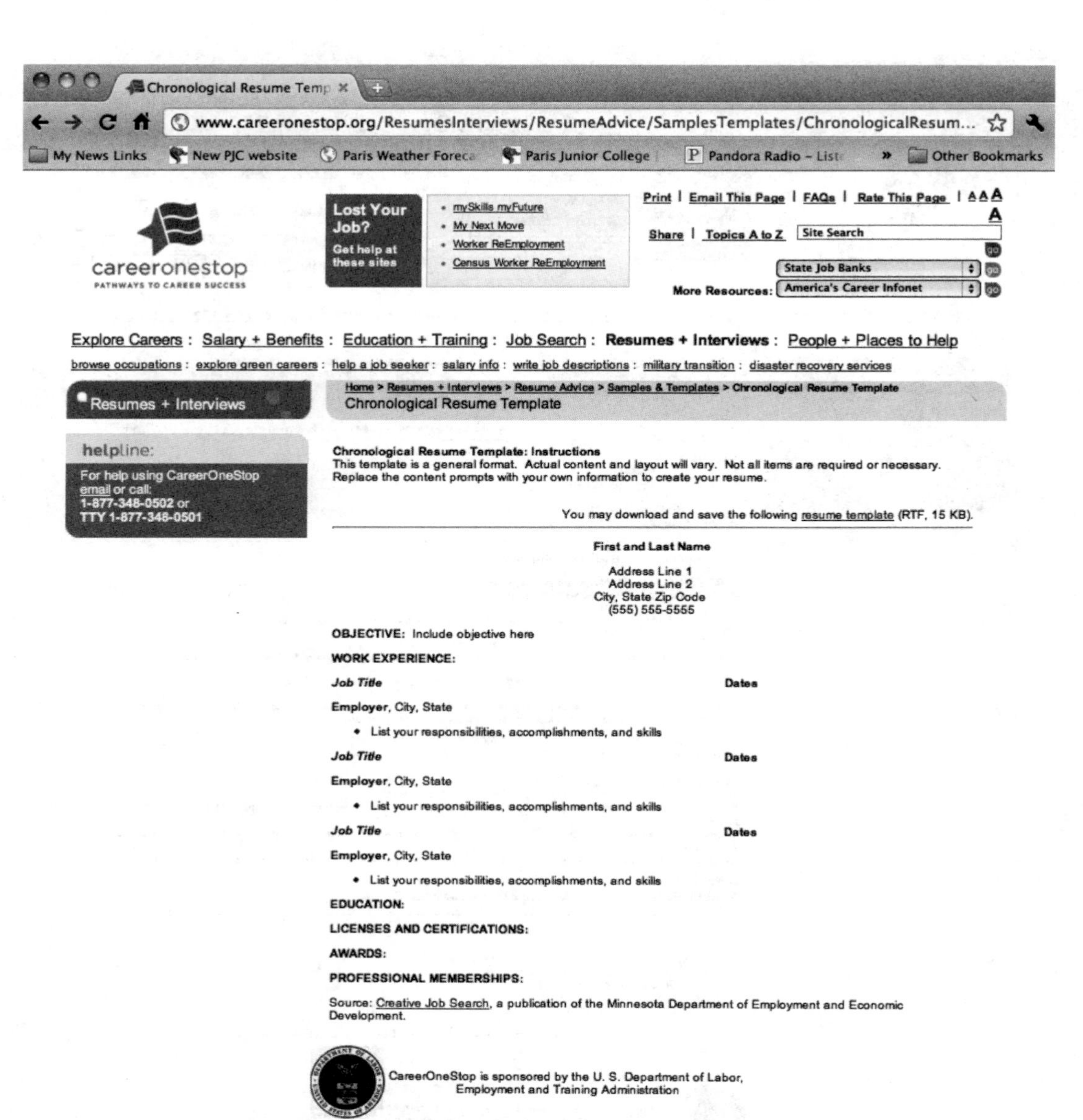

Chronological Resume Temp

www.careeronestop.org/ResumesInterviews/ResumeAdvice/SamplesTemplates/ChronologicalResum...

My News Links | New PJC website | Paris Weather Foreca | Paris Junior College | Pandora Radio - List | Other Bookmarks

careeronestop
PATHWAYS TO CAREER SUCCESS

Lost Your Job? Get help at these sites

- mySkills myFuture
- My Next Move
- Worker ReEmployment
- Census Worker ReEmployment

Print | Email This Page | FAQs | Rate This Page | A A A A

Share | Topics A to Z | Site Search

State Job Banks

More Resources: America's Career Infonet

Explore Careers : Salary + Benefits : Education + Training : Job Search : **Resumes + Interviews** : People + Places to Help

browse occupations : explore green careers : help a job seeker : salary info : write job descriptions : military transition : disaster recovery services

Resumes + Interviews

Home > Resumes + Interviews > Resume Advice > Samples & Templates > **Chronological Resume Template**

Chronological Resume Template

helpline:

For help using CareerOneStop email or call:
1-877-348-0502 or
TTY 1-877-348-0501

Chronological Resume Template: Instructions
This template is a general format. Actual content and layout will vary. Not all items are required or necessary. Replace the content prompts with your own information to create your resume.

You may download and save the following resume template (RTF, 15 KB).

First and Last Name

Address Line 1
Address Line 2
City, State Zip Code
(555) 555-5555

OBJECTIVE: Include objective here

WORK EXPERIENCE:

Job Title **Dates**

Employer, City, State

- List your responsibilities, accomplishments, and skills

Job Title **Dates**

Employer, City, State

- List your responsibilities, accomplishments, and skills

Job Title **Dates**

Employer, City, State

- List your responsibilities, accomplishments, and skills

EDUCATION:

LICENSES AND CERTIFICATIONS:

AWARDS:

PROFESSIONAL MEMBERSHIPS:

Source: Creative Job Search, a publication of the Minnesota Department of Employment and Economic Development.

CareerOneStop is sponsored by the U. S. Department of Labor, Employment and Training Administration

Home | Explore Careers | Salary + Benefits | Education + Training | Job Search | Resumes + Interviews | People + Places to Help
About Us | Site Privacy | Contact Us | Link to Us | Site Map | Copyright © 2011 State of Minnesota

Notes

NOTESLCT-08A1M

Notes

Notes

Notes

Notes

NOTESLCT-08A1M

Notes

Notes

Notes

Notes

Notes

Notes

Notes

Notes

Notes

Connections:

An Insider's Guide to College Success

INCLUDES 50 TIPS
PLANNING FOR COLLEGE SUCCESS

Printed on recyclable paper.
Web site: www.premier.us | www.premier.ca
E-mail: smile.psd@schoolspecialty.com

Table of Contents

Introduction 2

CHAPTER 1
Time Management 4

CHAPTER 2
Learning Styles 14

CHAPTER 3
Reading Skills 20

CHAPTER 4
Writing 28

CHAPTER 5
Diversity 40

CHAPTER 6
Taking Notes 54

CHAPTER 7
Developing Critical-Thinking Skills 64

CHAPTER 8
Studying For & Taking Tests 76

CHAPTER 9
Personal Planning & Goal-Setting 88

CHAPTER 10
Financial Responsibility 96

CHAPTER 11
Wellness 106

Planning Pages 134

If found, please return to:

NAME

ADDRESS

PHONE

INTRODUCTION

Connections:

An Insider's Guide to College Success is a unique manual designed specifically for students beginning their college journey.

Connections is just as much a resource guide as it is a textbook. It includes information, tips, and strategies designed to make your academic career and extracurricular interests more productive and enjoyable. Each chapter has been written with you in mind and is packed with information that can help you make a successful transition to college.

There are activities and reflection points in several sections of this manual. Take time to complete the reflections and goals in a thoughtful way. These sections are designed to facilitate progress in defining and reaching your personal and academic goals. Developing goals that are unique to your needs is a critical component of developing a comprehensive learning plan and is important to your success in college.

As you familiarize yourself with the wealth of information that is presented throughout the chapters, monthly themes, and 50 Tips for College Success, you will find that *Connections* is truly an *Insider's Guide to College Success*.

CHAPTER 1

Time Management

Getting Started: Knowing How You Spend Time

Most high school students have a planned and scripted daily time schedule, and there's little choice once the schedule is set.

In the college setting, there is considerably less arranged, scripted, and planned time. Students need to have good time-management skills in order to be successful college students.

Some students make the mistake of using their newfound freedom in college for partying and socializing to an unreasonable extent. Some of these students are not using their time optimally and effectively and have to learn new habits and patterns of time management. It is helpful to begin an analysis of your time usage by writing down everything you do for a week in one-hour blocks. Be specific and thorough. This process will demonstrate how you are spending the bulk of your time. It will undoubtedly show you areas in which you are wasting time.

Look at your weekly time report and be honest about areas of improvement. Keep an eye toward specific activities that "waste" lots of time. That could be social networking, talking on your phone, texting, and so on. Based on the findings, list the top five ways you could improve your time management below.

Top Five Ways I Could Improve My Time Management:

1. ....

2. ....

3. ....

4. ....

5. ....

Following an analysis of improving your time management, the next step is getting a system in place to help you organize your time. The planner part of this text is the perfect place to begin. The important thing is to find a system that works for you and assists you in planning to make the most of each day. You need to create the habit of using the time- planning/management tool daily. There are many online tools that can assist in this function. Use the system diligently, checking it throughout the day. Refine your tasks daily as necessary. Put everything you need for better time management in one planner location. Be proactive in planning your day, week, month, semester, year at college, and your entire college program/years. State below a summary of the system you will use to begin your time-management work. Study the system you will be using, if there is one in addition to the text planner. Although an electronic or online planner can have useful features, you may be unable to remember all of the daily entries when you are away from a computer. If this is the case, you may wish to print out your online schedule in addition to keeping it organized.

Think THIS WEEK'S GOALS, PROJECTS, IDEAS

Record ASSIGNMENTS & TESTS

Know Your Professors

They are key to your learning and college success.

At the first class meeting of the term, obtain and record the professor's office location and hours, email address, and phone number. Also get the names and contact information of at least two students in each of your classes so that you can ask for such things clarification of information presented in class, assignment questions and collaborations, notes for meetings you missed, and so on. Keep this material close at hand and save it in multiple locations.

142

AUGUST 2010

Act PLAN MY PRIORITIES

a.m. p.m.

16 monday

17 tuesday

18 wednesday

19 thursday

20 friday

21 saturday

22 sunday

Check REVIEW AND REFLECT ✓ Did I achieve my weekly goals? → What didn't get accomplished?

143

Time-Management Overview

Time-Management Tool(s) Selected:

How I Will Use this Tool to Help Me Improve Time Management:

Of course, the best time-management tools need to be used daily to be effective. This depends on the quality of the input—which depends on you! If you forget to record deadlines and assignments in a timely manner, the best planning system is useless. Getting organized is important and a good place to start. Determine systems and calendars you will use for each of the following needs:

Daily Calendar:

Weekly Calendar:

Monthly Calendar:

Semester Calendar:

Yearly Calendar:

Planning Calendar for College Years:

Establish a reliable system for recording important dates, classes, deadlines, projects, reading assignments, and exams for each class. Constantly review, refine, and update this information. Read your daily schedule prior to the start of each day. Also, read it at the end of the day and plan or make any needed changes. Update weekly calendars daily. Update monthly calendars at least weekly. Review semester calendars weekly as well, making any needed changes and adjustments. Make reminder notes of upcoming important work and fun events. Schedule downtime and other activities that may help you relieve stress. Schedule social time, but be realistic. Try to stick to your planned time periods and events. Know that there will always be a distraction around the corner in college life. It is important to learn to manage these distractions and still meet time-management goals.

In the area of planning your time, write a critique of how well you are doing and areas that need improvement. Look at the topics above and self-assess problem areas, as well as those in which you are doing well.

Think THIS WEEK'S GOALS, PROJECTS, IDEAS

Get folder for syllabi
Laundry
Finish financial aid apps
Write down test dates for semester

Record ASSIGNMENTS & TESTS

Set up Twitter account for English class by Wednesday

American History chap. 6 pgs 180-213

Group project outline due

Chem Quiz!

Post English discussion by midnight

Know Your Professors

They are key to your learning and college success.

At the first class meeting of the term, obtain and record the professor's office location and hours, email address, and phone number. Also get the names and contact information of at least two students in each of your classes so that you can ask for such things clarification of information presented in class, assignment questions and collaborations, notes for meetings you missed, and so on. Keep this material close at hand and save it in multiple locations.

142

AUGUST 2010

Act PLAN MY PRIORITIES

	a.m.	p.m.
16 monday	Insurance payment due!	
17 tuesday	Start research for Humanities paper	Finish group project outline for tomorrow
18 wednesday	Study for Chem quiz	Jesse's birthday
19 thursday		Astrology lab Meet at Science bldg 11PM
20 friday	Last day to drop classes	Miller Hall BBQ at 6PM
21 saturday	Western at MSU 7PM	
22 sunday		

Check REVIEW AND REFLECT ✔ Did I achieve my weekly goals? → What didn't get accomplished? 143

Personal Critique of How I Am Managing My Time.

Write honest responses to the categories below:

Studying for Classes: ……………………………………………………………………

……………………………………………………………………………………………

Class Work, Assignments, and Exams: ……………………………………………

……………………………………………………………………………………………

Clubs and Organizations: ………………………………………………………………

……………………………………………………………………………………………

Work Responsibilities: …………………………………………………………………

……………………………………………………………………………………………

Internships, etc.: …………………………………………………………………………

……………………………………………………………………………………………

Social Time: ………………………………………………………………………………

……………………………………………………………………………………………

Time Wasters: ……………………………………………………………………………

……………………………………………………………………………………………

Friends: ……………………………………………………………………………………

……………………………………………………………………………………………

Family: ……………………………………………………………………………………

……………………………………………………………………………………………

Summary of areas where I can improve use of my time: ………………………

……………………………………………………………………………………………

……………………………………………………………………………………………

……………………………………………………………………………………………

……………………………………………………………………………………………

……………………………………………………………………………………………

Time-Management Practical Tips:

There is often a positive relationship between the time management of college students and the ability to be organized and efficient. Make sure you work on both areas together. There are a number of specific tips that are helpful to students in using their time to their best advantage. Read and reflect on the list that follows:

1. *Constantly review and prioritize your work and tasks. List the top three things you need to do at the beginning of the day. Make a daily To-Do list.*
2. *Start the day with the most difficult tasks. You should be fresher and more prepared for these tasks at the top of the morning.*
3. *Work ahead; don't procrastinate. Never wait until the last minute to begin or complete an assignment.*
4. *Pace yourself. Take short breaks. This should help increase the oxygen flow to your brain and help you to do better quality work.*
5. *When working on the computer, plan times to look away from the screen and walk away from the computer. Be sure to place yourself in an ergonomically correct position.*
6. *Before starting an assignment or project, make certain you understand the assignment expectations. Clarify this information well in advance of starting the work.*
7. *Plan your day in one-hour blocks. Outline each task of the day using this system. Build in some flex time.*
8. *Have a peer or mentor review your time-management plans. Ask this person for feedback. How can you improve your time-management plans?*

9. *Always have work at hand. Think about how you can get small amounts of work completed during typical down times. For example, when washing clothes, commuting, etc.*

10. *Everyone has the same hours in a day. How well are you using your time? Are there others around you, such as peers, mentors, or faculty, from whom you can learn how to better manage your time?*

11. *Plan for the unexpected and allow some time each day for the spontaneous to occur.*

12. *Take time for things that reduce your stress on a daily basis. Find out what works for you.*

13. *Always keep a watch, phone, or other device that has the time ready at hand. Be aware of the time and your schedule for the day on an hourly basis.*

14. *Review, re-check, and reflect on your work. Complete your work early enough so you have time for each of these three steps.*

15. *Consider your schoolwork to be a full-time job. You need two to three hours of outside study prior and after each class period.*

16. *Carefully consider the impact of having a job outside of class. Some students work too many hours to be able to adequately complete their college obligations.*

17. *Spend time and effort locating places to study that are conducive to work and concentration.*

18. *Be aware of distractions that can take away your time, concentration, and motivation to study. Stay focused and don't allow distractions to keep you from getting your work completed.*

19. *Post your time-management improvement goals where you can see them routinely. Make sure you have a plan to improve your use of time.*

20. *Use library resources to be more efficient in your research and classwork assignments. Get to know the skills and abilities of the research librarians.*
21. *Keep a notebook and pencil/pen with you at all times, so you can write your thoughts and ideas down.*
22. *Turn off the TV, computer, etc.,—whatever takes too much of your time for too little return.*
23. *Plan large projects by working backwards. With a calendar, note the date the project is due and work backwards, identifying details until starting dates and tasks are identified.*
24. *Set and schedule rewards for yourself for completing work on time and of high quality.*
25. *Give your largest effort to the work that has the most important payoff and provides long-term benefits.*

Now review the tips and determine which ones you most need to concentrate on to improve your time-management skills. Take a highlighter and mark the ones you need to continue to think about and revisit.

Goals to Improve My Time-Management Skills:

Choose five goals from the previous list to improve your practice of time-management skills. Write the list below:

Goal 1: ....

....

....

....

Goal 2: ....

....

....

....

Goal 3: ....

....

....

....

Goal 4: ....

....

....

....

Goal 5: ....

....

....

....

Be sure to post and display your goals where you can refer to them often. Think about specific ways you can meet the goals.

You can also identify ways to improve your learning by recognizing the learning styles that are less comfortable for you, and developing skills to help you improve in these areas.

CHAPTER 2

Learning Styles

Learning styles classify the method through which you best learn and approach new concepts.

You may receive information best through visual, auditory, or kinesthetic processes, or a combination of these methods. Understanding how you comprehend information is the first step to developing study strategies that work for you. Once you have identified how you process information, you can identify the most effective study methods for your style.

Identifying Your Learning Style

Before you can identify the study strategies that will work best for you, you must identify your learning style. You likely already know a good deal about your preferred method of learning. Consider the types of environments where you can effectively comprehend presented information and the environments that are the most challenging.

These questions may help you identify your learning style. Note the learning style that you are most likely to answer "yes" to.

AUDITORY

- *Are you able to remember the lyrics to a song after hearing it only one or two times?*
- *Do you prefer classes when lecture is the primary method that information is shared between instructors and students?*
- *Do you often create songs, rhymes, or stories to help you remember important concepts?*

Tips For Auditory Learners

- *Attend class regularly. You are more likely to remember information when it is shared verbally; therefore, hearing class lectures and discussions is key.*
- *Read your notes out loud into a recorder and listen to the recording as part of your test preparation.*
- *Ask your professor if you can record class lectures. Replaying the lectures may help you organize and fill in any gaps in your notes.*
- *Discuss new concepts with your classmates. Explaining ideas to your peers may help you better understand the information.*

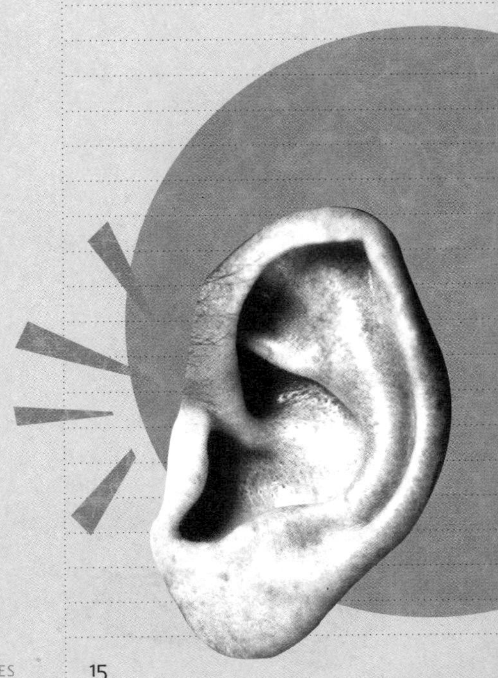

VISUAL

- *When you are assembling an item of furniture, do you refer to the pictures and diagrams included with the instructions?*
- *Are your notes organized and neat? Do you supplement your written notes with diagrams or graphic depictions of the presented information? Do you use different colored ink or highlighters to distinguish between concepts?*
- *When taking a test or quiz, are you able to visualize your notes and recall information based on where it appeared on the pages?*

Tips For Visual Learners

- *Use highlighters, colored ink, or underlining techniques to identify key concepts in your notes.*
- *Identify images to supplement any written information. Include these images in your notes to help make connections and remember important concepts.*
- *Use specific arrangements to help organize your notes. For example, use the margins to note vocabulary words, and/or save the bottom third of the page for questions you want to follow up on.*
- *When you are taking an exam, visualize your notes and study guide to help you recall information.*

READ/WRITE

- *If a professor uses a Power Point presentation, do you prefer to print the slides ahead of time and use that as a guide for your notes?*
- *When you are preparing for a quiz or exam, do you rewrite your notes?*
- *Do you find that completing the assigned reading before class helps you to understand what is presented in class?*

Tips For Read/Write Learners

- *Complete any assigned reading before attending the lecture. This will help you connect what you read with what is being said, and make the presented information seem more familiar.*
- *Rewrite your in-class notes and combine them with the notes you take from your assigned reading. Then, read and reread your class notes each day to aid in your memorization and understanding of the information.*
- *Explain diagrams and graphs with statements to be sure you understand what the images represent.*
- *Create practice tests and quiz yourself on information using flash cards.*

KINESTHETIC

- *When you are assembling an item of furniture, do you ignore the included instructions and jump right into the assembly?*
- *Do you prefer classes when you have the opportunity to experiment and practice the presented information over courses when lecture is the primary learning format?*
- *When you are in class, do you find yourself tapping your fingers, bouncing your leg up and down, or doodling on your notes?*

Tips For Kinesthetic Learners

- *Identify situations in which the presented material may be applied in your life. Additionally, make note of any examples or scenarios that the professor offers.*
- *Choose courses that supplement class sessions with laboratories or recitations. These sessions are often taught in smaller groups and use hands-on teaching techniques.*
- *Take field trips to help make the connection between your coursework and its application to the world.*
- *As you prepare for an exam, refer to your previous tests for that class or ask the professor to share the format of the questions. Then, create practice tests for yourself using that format.*

Developing Effective Study Strategies

Identifying your learning preferences can help you develop effective strategies to prepare for class, organize your course materials, and, ultimately, do your best on class assignments and exams. Additionally, you can identify strategies that may help you develop your ability to learn in a variety of environments. It is likely that during your college career, you will enroll in a course in which the professor uses a teaching style that is not aligned with your preferred learning style. If you are a kinesthetic learner, for example, you may find yourself distracted or disinterested in lecture courses. If you prefer to learn through reading and writing, you may be challenged by a laboratory course in which you have to practice concepts through hands-on processes rather than learning from texts or notes. Understanding effective strategies for each learning style can help you adapt and be successful in a diverse array of learning environments.

Conclusion

You likely have some study habits that you developed in high school that work well for you. There are probably other methods that worked for you in the past but that you have not been as successful with since starting college-level work. Recognizing how you best learn and challenging yourself to develop new strategies and enhance the strategies you already practice will help you create environments where you can maximize your learning potential. When you find yourself in a challenging course, try to identify the learning style that may help you thrive in that environment and consider new or different study strategies than what you typically practice. As you build a deeper understanding of your learning style, you may find that you are able to employ a variety of study skills depending on the environment and the type of information you are learning.

CHAPTER 3

Reading Skills

Have you ever sat down to complete a reading assignment and found that after reading a full page, you had no idea what you just read?

Effectively reading and understanding new information is a challenge for many students. Your assigned readings are often from textbooks or scholarly journals that are formatted in a way that is quite different from the texts you used in high school.

You likely will be expected to complete a larger amount of reading in a shorter amount of time in college. Additionally, professors may not tell you exactly what concepts from the reading are most important. Developing effective reading skills is a critical component of becoming a successful college student. There are methods you can practice to help you get the most from your time spent reading.

When you are developing your study plan, it is important you include time to complete your readings. Even if professors do not quiz you on assigned readings, they expect you to complete them in preparation for class. Often, lectures are used to supplement the assigned readings and, without a thorough understanding of the material, you may not understand the in-class lecture. The amount of time needed to complete a reading assignment varies with each student. The rate at which you can read and understand new material will differ from your peers. When determining how much time you should plan to complete your reading, consider not only how many pages you are expected to complete but also the rate at which you read and understand new material. For example, it may be unreasonable for you to expect to complete 100 pages of reading in a 30-minute period. However, if you have the attention span to read for 30 uninterrupted minutes, you will need to plan enough 30-minute sessions to complete the reading in time to complete your assignment or prepare for your class.

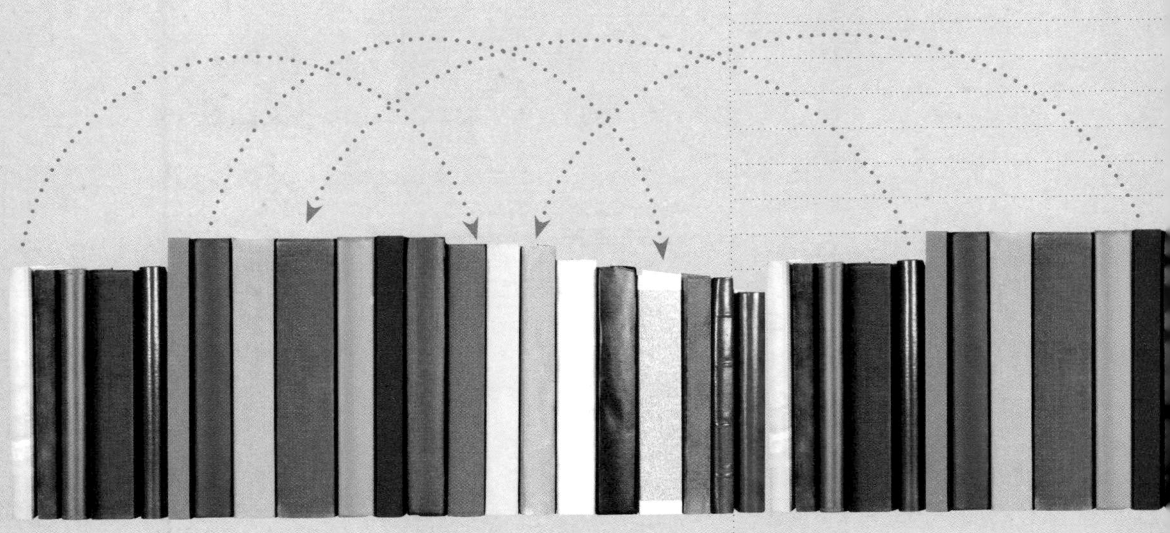

Reading with the SQ3R Method

When you are completing your reading assignments, make the most of your time. For over 60 years, students have been practicing effective reading skills using the SQ3R method, developed by Francis Robinson (1941). The SQ3R method will help you develop effective reading habits by practicing the steps of:

Survey
Question
Read
Recite
Review

Before you begin reading, *survey* the material. Begin with the table of contents and title and identify the concepts being presented. Scan the pages making note of the headings and subheadings. Familiarize yourself with the author's use of footnotes or references. Note any use of bold or italicized words—this may indicate that they are key concepts. Review the illustrations, graphs, and photos used to supplement the narrative.

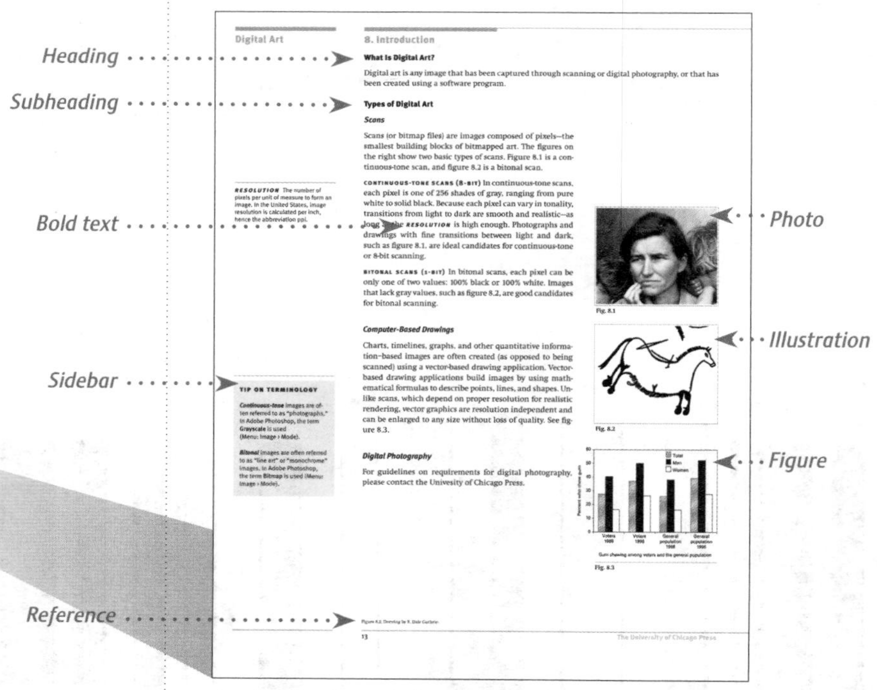

Digital Art

8. Introduction

What Is Digital Art?

Digital art is any image that has been captured through scanning or digital photography, or that has been created using a software program.

Types of Digital Art

Scans

Scans (or bitmap files) are images composed of pixels—the smallest building blocks of bitmapped art. The figures on the right show two basic types of scans. Figure 8.1 is a continuous-tone scan, and figure 8.2 is a bitonal scan.

CONTINUOUS-TONE SCANS (8-BIT) In continuous-tone scans, each pixel is one of 256 shades of gray, ranging from pure white to solid black. Because each pixel can vary in tonality, transitions from light to dark are smooth and realistic—as long [illegible] ***RESOLUTION*** is high enough. Photographs and drawings with fine transitions between light and dark, such as figure 8.1, are ideal candidates for continuous-tone or 8-bit scanning.

BITONAL SCANS (1-BIT) In bitonal scans, each pixel can be only one of two values: 100% black or 100% white. Images that lack gray values, such as figure 8.2, are good candidates for bitonal scanning.

RESOLUTION The number of pixels per unit of measure to form an image. In the United States, image resolution is calculated per inch, hence the abbreviation ppi.

Computer-Based Drawings

Charts, timelines, graphs, and other quantitative information–based images are often created (as opposed to being scanned) using a vector-based drawing application. Vector-based drawing applications build images by using mathematical formulas to describe points, lines, and shapes. Unlike scans, which depend on proper resolution for realistic rendering, vector graphics are resolution independent and can be enlarged to any size without loss of quality. See figure 8.3.

TIP ON TERMINOLOGY

Continuous-tone images are often referred to as "photographs." In Adobe Photoshop, the term **Grayscale** is used (Menu: Image › Mode).

Bitonal images are often referred to as "line art" or "monochrome" images. In Adobe Photoshop, the term **Bitmap** is used (Menu: Image › Mode).

Digital Photography

For guidelines on requirements for digital photography, please contact the Univesity of Chicago Press.

Fig. 8.1

Fig. 8.2

Fig. 8.3

Figure 8.2: Drawing by S. Dale Guthrie

13

The University of Chicago Press

Reprinted with permission from the University of Chicago Press.

After you have surveyed the material, ask *questions* to help you begin to formulate opinions about the presented concepts. We interpret information based on previous experiences, so start by asking yourself, "What do I already know about this topic?" and, "How will I be able to apply this information to my life?" Write down questions you have about each section of the reading, based on what you surveyed of the headings and key words. Formulating questions before you begin reading will help you think more critically about the material and give you a purpose for reading.

After surveying and questioning, you are ready to read the material. You should read at a speed that allows you to comprehend important information. As you are reading, stop after each section and ask yourself, "Did I understand this section?" If you are able to summarize the material in your own words, you are likely ready to begin reading the next section. If you are not clear, reread the material before moving on. Practice active-reading strategies such as highlighting key terms, using your own words to summarize concepts, and noting connections to your class notes and other course materials.

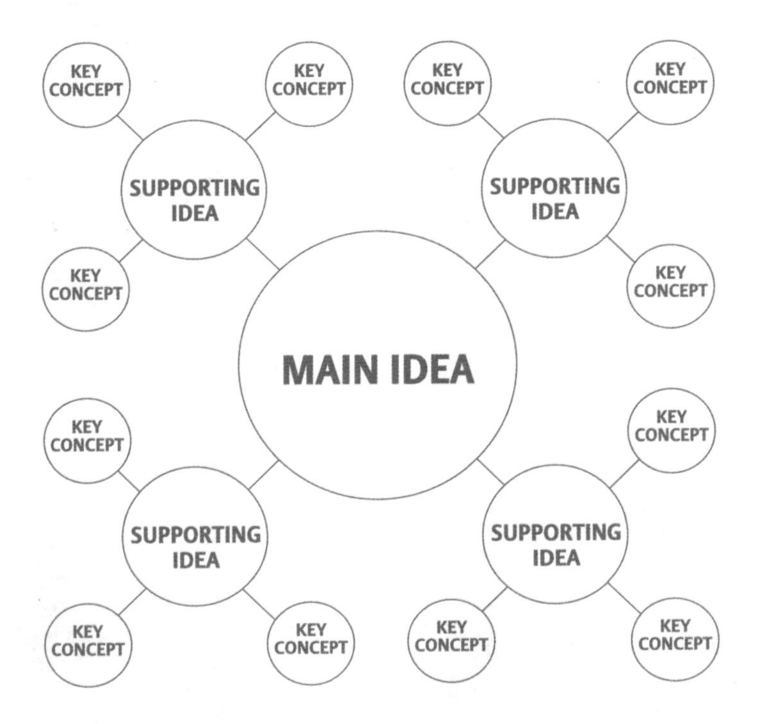

Mapping

Textbook chapters or sections often contain a large amount of information on a topic. *Information is often presented in a sequence that allows the reader to build upon ideas from previous sections or chapters. Mapping is an active-reading strategy that allows you to create a visual representation of the information. It is an effort to help you understand how various concepts are connected. Through mapping you can also make connections between what you are currently reading and what you already know about the topic.*

One way to gauge your understanding of the material is to try to recite what you have read. Once you have read the material, put the contents into your own words. Summarize the material in writing or explain it to a study partner. Reciting with a partner and comparing notes can help you identify any discrepancies in how you interpreted the reading. You may also refer back to the questions you formulated in the second step and try to answer them.

After completing the assignment, continue to review the material and your notes. When you read simply for the purpose of checking off an assignment for that week, you most likely will be unable to recall the information after a day, a week, or in two weeks when you need it for an exam. Regular review of your reading will help retain and more fully comprehend the information.

By practicing the SQ3R method, you will not only be able to recall the information that you read, but you will more fully understand the content and how it applies to other concepts you are learning. You will also find that if you review course material regularly, you can avoid the stress that comes with cramming for an exam. It will be easier to prepare for tests since you will simply be refreshing your memory, as opposed to trying to learn a large amount of new information in a short period of time.

Memory Curve

As illustrated in the graph below, as time passes, you are able to recall less of what you read. *This is because you commit new information to your short-term memory when you first read it. As you review the information, however, you begin to more thoroughly understand the material and it becomes part of your long-term memory.*

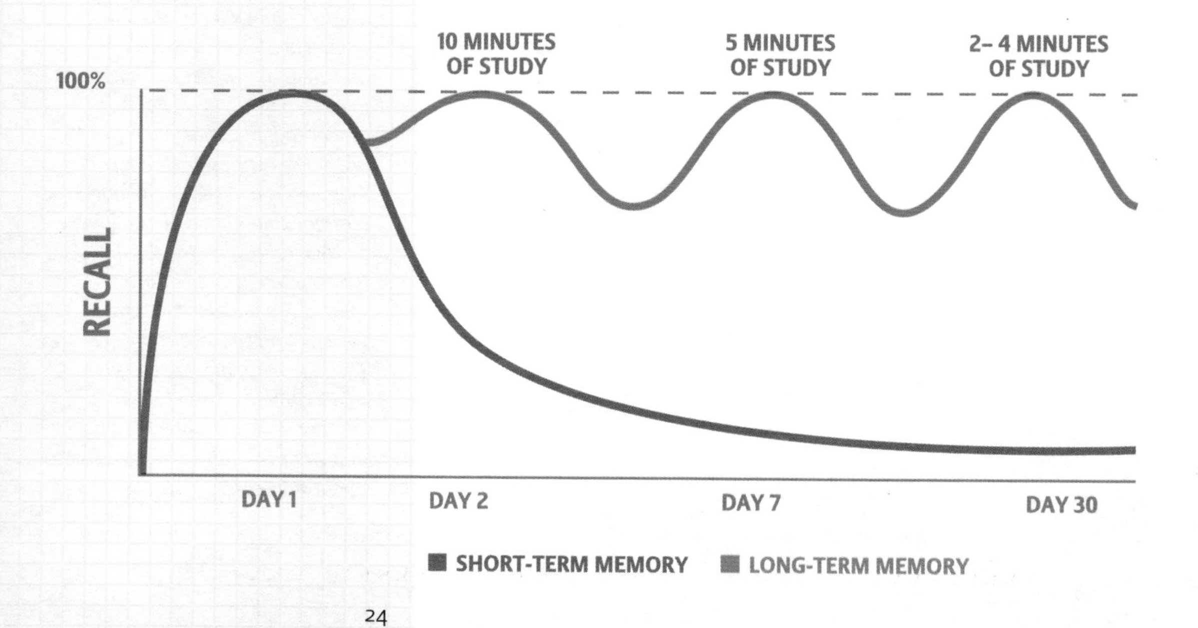

Make the Most of Your Reading

- ***Avoid cramming all of the assigned reading right before an exam.*** *Doing this does not allow you time to comprehend and understand the material. Make the most of your time and practice the SQ3R method to ensure you comprehend and can recall and apply what you have read.*
- ***Be an active reader.*** *Taking notes while reading can increase your comprehension of the material, as well as help you prepare for assignments and exams where you may need to apply what you read. Use your margins and annotate what you have read, using your own words. Create note cards with key concepts that you can use to quiz yourself. Write down questions you may have about the reading and share those questions with your professor or study group.*
- ***Stay focused.*** *Reading without focus is a waste of your time. When you prepare to complete a reading assignment, consider your environment. Are you free from interruptions? Is the environment quiet? Are you prepared to focus on your assignment for at least a 30-minute span of time? You will be a more effective and more efficient reader if you work in an environment with minimal distractions. If you find yourself "zoning out," take a break. You want to be sure you are not only seeing the words on the page but are actually reading and understanding the information.*

Tips

Identify support programs your college offers for students who would like some assistance developing effective reading habits. *If English is not your native language, if you have a reading disability, or if you would like to increase the pace at which you read and understand material, there are strategies you can use to help improve your reading skills. Recognizing areas where you may need assistance is an important part of becoming a successful college student.*

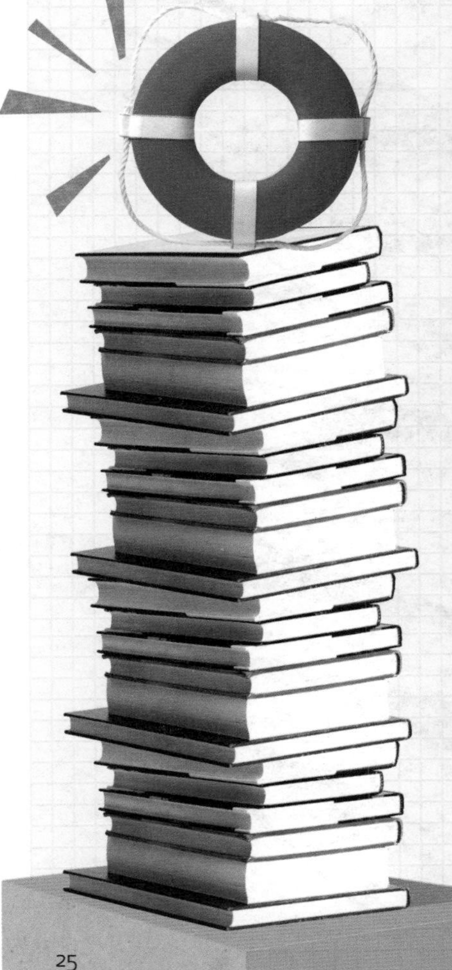

- ***Look up unfamiliar words and terms.*** *If you come across a term that you do not know, pause from your reading and look up the definition. It is a good idea to have a dictionary or access to an online dictionary such as www.merriam-webster.com as part of your study materials. Looking up new terms as you are reading will help you put them into the proper context and will help clarify the meaning of the text.*
- ***Review the text regularly.*** *The more often you review the text, the more fully you will comprehend the material. It is good practice to highlight or underline key topics in the reading to help you easily identify the most important concepts when reviewing the text.*

Conclusion

Becoming an effective reader is a learning process and may take some time. You may find that your ability to quickly understand the readings in some courses differs from your ability to understand material in others. This can be contributed to many factors such as your interest in the topic (the more interested you are in a subject, the easier it will be to complete and understand the readings), your ability to apply the readings to your previous experiences, and the format in which the material is presented. As you practice the SQ3R strategy, you will become a faster, more effective reader. Allow yourself ample time to complete assigned readings, and remember to be flexible with your active-reading practices as you may find what works for one type of text may not work with others.

Reference

Robinson, F.P. (1941). *Effective behavior*. New York: Harper & Row.

CHAPTER 4

Writing

Writing as a Learning Process

In his book, *On Writing Well*, William Zinsser wrote "the act of writing gives the teacher a window into the mind of the student" (2001).

Throughout your college experience you will be expected to demonstrate your understanding of a topic through written assignments.

Unlike exams, writing a paper challenges you to organize your ideas on paper and to make connections between multiple concepts so the professor will know that you fully understand the material being covered. Written assignments also allow you to delve deeper into topics that may interest you. For example, if you are enrolled in an Introduction to World Religion course, your instructor may spend only a few days on Middle Eastern religions. A term paper would allow you to further explore this area of religion or any other area that interests you. Writing assignments range from very informal, such as a two-minute free writing assignment at the start of class, to more formal assignments, such as a lengthy research paper. It is important to understand that written assignments are not only part of your English courses but a component of most of your courses, whether you are submitting a formal term paper or a laboratory report.

Many students dread writing papers and state that they would rather study for a test. If this is true for you, consider the benefits of written assignments. There is much less pressure than an exam situation, you are allowed more time to prepare your final product, and you have the opportunity to use many resources, unlike when taking an exam. When writing a paper you also have the ability to get help from elsewhere such as the campus writing center, your professor, or peers who are skilled in editing and proofreading. Unlike when you are asked to demonstrate your knowledge on an exam, you are in full control of what you submit via a written assignment. If you plan accordingly and adhere to the writing process presented in this chapter, you may find yourself enjoying the process of writing.

The Importance of Writing Well

Your ability to write, and write well, is often used to determine your acceptance to a position or organization. You may have submitted a writing sample as part of your college application if you were asked to submit a personal statement or respond to an essay prompt. The SAT and GRE exams, which are commonly used to determine college and graduate school admissions, contain a written portion. Additionally, many scholarship applications include a writing component, either as an essay response or submitted writing sample, to help determine the most qualified applicants. Furthermore, it is important that you develop and refine your writing skills as you prepare for your career. There are few professions where you will not be expected to communicate via written word, whether through the exchange of e-mail, submitted reports, press announcements, or research-based proposals. You may be asked, as part of your application process, to submit a sample of your best writing or complete a writing test as part of the interview process. High-quality writing skills are an essential part of displaying that you are a well-educated individual.

Types of Writing

You will have many opportunities throughout your college career to practice and improve your writing skills. You may be asked to write informal essays, which are short writing assignments often open to personal opinion or bias, that may or may not require you to consult outside resources to support your ideas. Another type of writing is the persuasive essay, in which you take a stance about a topic and use a combination of facts and opinion to build arguments that will convince your reader to agree with your reasoning. Many professors will require you to submit reaction papers in which you react to an event (for example, attending a theater performance or cultural event) and make connections between your experience and your course material. Reaction papers allow you to interject your opinion as they are based on your unique experience.

More formal writing assignments may be based exclusively on factual information. For example, you may be asked to submit a laboratory report about an experiment you conduct in your science lab. This type of writing requires you to recount a series of events and draw conclusions about the experience based on what you have learned in class. A different type of fact-based report, and the type of writing that many students find the most daunting, is the formal research-based paper. In a research assignment, you are expected to identify and familiarize yourself with information about a particular topic, then present the information in an organized manner while adhering to specific formatting and citation guidelines.

With such a variety of writing assignments, it is imperative that you make note of the specific instructions provided to you and ensure that you understand what the professor expects. Once you have a clear understanding of the assignment, you can plan accordingly for the amount of time you expect the assignment to take and start collecting information for your paper.

The Writing Process: Prewriting, Writing, Rewriting

Submitting your best work on a paper is the final step in a process of developing and preparing your writing assignment. In order to ensure you submit your best work, it is important that you engage fully in each step of the writing process: prewriting, writing, and rewriting. Many students make the mistake of starting a writing assignment with a first draft and make little to no changes from the first to the final draft. Much like preparing for an exam, writing a paper does not *effectively* happen in one sitting. When you rush through a writing assignment and neglect the important steps of the writing process, you submit an unfinished paper and most often will find that your grade reflects your rushed attitude toward the assignment.

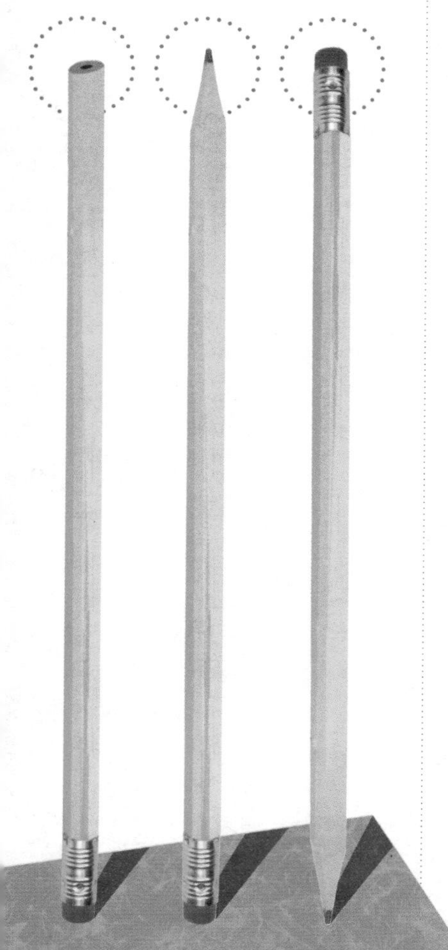

As you gain experience writing college-level papers, you will begin to develop your own style of paper preparation and execution. You will also become more confident with your writing and develop your own writing style. As a new college writer, adhere to the three-step writing process and you will find that you are able to develop strong papers that reflect well-developed thoughts and ideas; and as Zinsser stated, allow your professor to see what you are thinking.

PREWRITING

The first and most important step of the writing process is prewriting or planning. During this stage, you will do little to no writing of complete sentences but rather focus on selecting your topic, gathering and organizing your resources, and outlining the ideas you want to include in your paper. You should spend the **most** time in the prewriting stage. A common mistake student writers make is speeding through the prewriting stage and going directly into the writing stage. Consider, instead, the many things you can do to prepare for a more effective writing session.

Steps for Effective Prewriting

- ***Select Your Topic.*** *When selecting a topic to focus on for your assignment, consider what most interests you about the subject area. It is important you select a topic that you are enthusiastic about, or that you at least can remain interested for the duration of the assignment. The more interested you are in your topic, the more motivated you will be to complete the work. Your topic should be manageable; narrow enough that you can cover the material in the allotted length of the assignment, but broad enough that you are able to find relevant sources. If necessary, report your selection to your professor to ensure it meets the requirements of the assignment. Even if you are not required to get approval of your topic, clarify any questions you have about the assignment with your professor before you finalize your topic. It would be frustrating to begin work on your paper and learn later that you misunderstood the assignment and, therefore, have to revise your selection.*
- ***Record Your Ideas.*** *Once you have selected your topic, record what you already know about this subject matter, as well as any questions you hope to answer through your research. You may want to capture these ideas through a free-writing exercise in which you write all that you know about this topic and what most intrigues you about the subject. Brainstorm these ideas quickly and freely, without regard for sentence structure or grammar. Another strategy is to divide your paper into two columns, listing what you know about the topic on one side and the questions you have about it on the other side. This brainstorming session can be an effective way to begin your writing process as it helps you determine the questions you are seeking to answer through the gathering of sources.*

- ***Collect Your Resources.*** *Use your brainstorming results to help you get started in your collection of information. You may find resources in a variety of places, including your textbook, campus library, online journals, news articles, dissertations and theses, and primary sources. Do not be daunted by the task of identifying resources. Reference librarians can be wonderful resources and can help orient you to your institution's library and assist you in getting started with your research. As you find relevant sources, note the references within each source. You will often find that the bibliography of one source will help you identify other sources that may fit your topic. Be sure to note the requirements for your assignment when you are evaluating your resources. Your professor may specify the number and type of resources you should use.*
- ***Organize and Outline.*** *When you find a resource that fits your topic, make a few notes about the source, including the quality of the source, its relevance to your topic, and any key chapters or sections that are significant. This process is called "annotating" your sources and will help you recall why you selected each source once you begin writing, as well as assist you in staying organized with your sources. Include in your annotation the citation information including the title, author, publisher, and location and year of publication so you can accurately cite any sources you later use in your paper.*

Once you have collected and annotated a few sources, you are ready to outline your paper. The outlining process allows you to organize your ideas and the facts you have found through your resource collection into a logical order that can be expanded into paragraph form during the writing stage. Your outline should contain a few major topics or headings followed by the details that support or explain each idea. A thorough outline serves as the skeleton of your paper, proving the structure and support for your ideas before they become complete sentences.

Evaluating Information Sources

With so many media hosting information on endless topics, it can be difficult to determine the validity and, in some cases, the truth, in what you are reading. Identifying scholarly information sources is an important skill to learn. There are several things you can look for to help you determine the credibility of a source.

- ***Author information.*** *Note the author's name and credentials. Is this author affiliated with an organization or governmental department that would indicate expertise in the topic area? Can you identify other sources by the same author? First-time authors may very well be credible, but a history of publication on a particular topic would indicate a higher level of credibility than an author who was unknown in the subject area.*
- ***Publishing information.*** *Universities and colleges often have publishing presses. If your source comes from an academic institution, it is likely credible. You can verify the credibility of other publishers based on the amount of work they have produced on the topic and their reputation in the field you are studying. If you are unsure about a publisher's reputation, ask your professor. He or she is likely well-read in the content of your course and can help you identify some key publishers in the field.*
- ***Currency of the source.*** *How current is the publication? Is it the most up-to-date information? Many sources will have several editions—identify if you are using the most current edition. This is often difficult to tell on Web sites but is usually noted with the publishing information in print sources.*

Writing Through E-Mail

The use of electronic communication has enhanced the way we exchange information with one another. *You no longer have to wait for a class session to ask your professor a question thanks to the availability of e-mail. It is important to remember, however, that while it is convenient to send a quick text message to a friend or update your Twitter status using abbreviated language, when you are exchanging messages with your professors or other campus administrators, you should use a more formal style of communicating.*

(CONT'D)

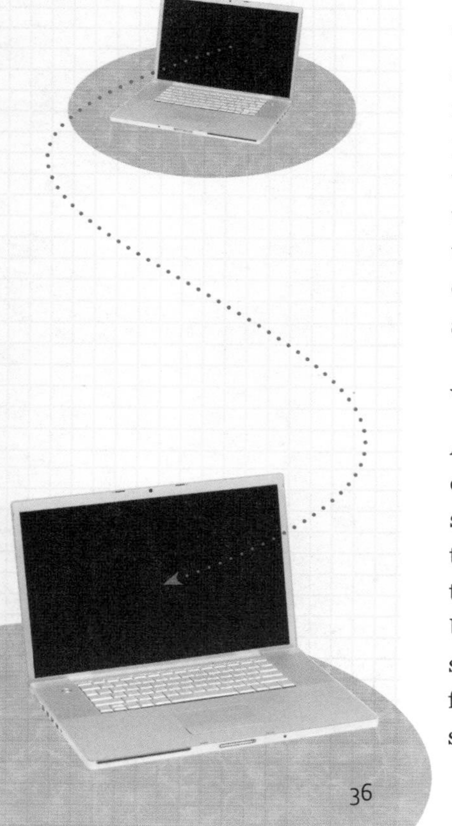

- ***Type of publication.*** *Journal articles, magazines, newspapers, books, and Web pages have various ways of being published. Some Web pages, like Wikipedia, are open access, allowing authors to post without much regard for fact verification. Web pages may also be authored by scholars who have a background in a particular area and can offer credible information about a topic. Popular magazines provide information on various subjects but would be seen as less credible than a peer-reviewed journal. For example,* Entertainment Weekly *magazine would be a good resource for someone who was interested in television and film. However,* Journal of Popular Film and Television *would be a better source for finding information to include in a term paper. The type of publication and the audience that the publication is written toward can help you determine the scholarly value of a source.*

There is no perfect formula for determining the validity of a source. Some Web pages contain scholarly information, and not all printed books would meet the criteria for a scholarly publication. As a researcher and writer, you can evaluate the validity of a source using these strategies. If you doubt the quality of a source, do not include it in your paper. With the wealth of information that is readily available through college and university libraries, you can find many valid sources to help support your writing.

WRITING

After you identify your topic, collect relevant sources and outline your ideas—you are ready to begin writing! You should begin writing your paper with the understanding that this will not be the final draft. A well-written paper goes through many revisions before it is ready for submission. Using your outline as your guide, expand your ideas into sentences that support your thesis. Do not worry about formatting and grammar issues during your first writing session. It is most important that you focus on the content of your paper, capture your ideas in a logical sequence, and support your claims with the information you found in your sources. You can clean up the formatting during the revision stage.

Recognizing and Avoiding Plagiarism

You are encouraged to learn through examining the ideas of others. For example, the process of writing a research paper includes gathering information that has been written or shared by others, and using their thoughts to formulate and support your own ideas. We often rely on the ideas of others to help us formulate our own thoughts. When you use the ideas of others, and give them credit for their work, you are practicing good research and writing skills.

When you do not give proper credit for the ideas or writing of others, it is considered plagiarism. As a college-level learner, you are expected to know what constitutes plagiarism, and to practice proper citation of your sources in your academic work. Professional organizations provide various guidelines for citing sources within the text as well as in a bibliography, reference page, or footnote citations. Your instructor will likely indicate the style guidelines you are expected to follow (i.e., APA, MLA, Chicago).

Some information is considered common knowledge and does not need to be cited (e.g., the Nile River is in Egypt). However, when you begin to state more specific facts (e.g., the length of the Nile River), you should note where you found your information. In addition to citing factual information, you must also remember to give credit to the ideas of others. Even if you are paraphrasing and not directly quoting the work of someone, you must credit his or her ideas.

When you annotate your sources, it helps to reduce the risk of plagiarism. When you find a source you want to use in your paper, summarize the information you read. Then, when you incorporate this source into your assignment, use the notes you made rather than the actual source. Be sure to give credit to the source, even if you did not use an exact quote.

Plan ahead for your assignments so you have the time to properly identify and credit your sources. When you wait

Remember these tips when you are e-mailing faculty and staff:

- *Include a subject line that informs the reader of your purpose:*
  Clarification on reaction paper assignment, English 101.
- *Use the e-mail address your institution provides rather than a Google-mail or Yahoo account (this will help keep your message from being flagged as spam).*
- *Write in complete sentences, but keep your message concise.*
- *An e-mail is not the proper medium to offer excuses for missed classes or late assignments. You may want to set up an appointment, via e-mail, to meet with the professor to explain any personal situations that have affected your classwork or attendance.*
- *Proofread your e-mail before you press "send," making sure to correct any misspellings.*
- *Avoid text-style abbreviations such as "thx," or "ttyl":*
  Thank you for responding with further clarification about this assignment. I will see you in class Tuesday.
- *Include a closing salutation with your name and course number/section:*
  Sincerely,
  Jane Thompson ENGL 101
  Section 004.
- *Do not expect an immediate response from your professor. While you may be thinking about your assignment at 2 a.m., it may take some time for the professor to get back to you.*

until the last minute to write a paper, you have less time to formulate your own ideas and, therefore, may be tempted to use the ideas of others as your own.

It is safe to practice this rule of citation: "When in doubt, cite!"

REWRITING

It is best not to revise your paper immediately after you complete the first draft. Take a break from your work and come back to it when you are feeling refreshed and ready for a second look at what you wrote. During the revision, you can look more critically at organization and presentation of your ideas. In the first revision, focus on editing for content rather than proofreading for formatting and grammar issues. You may want to ask yourself questions about the paper such as:

- *Did I engage the reader with a strong introduction?*
- *Have I clearly stated my thesis?*
- *Do the major ideas presented throughout the paper support the thesis?*
- *Is each idea supported with facts and details?*
- *Did I use transitions to help the reader understand the connection between ideas?*
- *Have I balanced the use of ideas from others to support my claims, while demonstrating that I understand that material by presenting original thoughts about the topic?*
- *Does my conclusion support my thesis and summarize the major ideas of the paper?*

Once you make the first round of adjustments to your content, take another break. In a second revision session, you can focus on proofreading your paper, noting any formatting or grammatical errors. Consider questions such as:

- *Have I given proper credit for any ideas that are not my own?*
- *Are my sources properly cited?*

- *Do I meet the requirements of the assignment? (i.e. the correct number and type of sources; margin size; font specifications; page length)*
- *What spelling or punctuation errors do I need to correct?*
- *Is the bibliography properly organized and accurate?*

After you have edited and proofread your paper, have someone from your campus writing center review your work. Sometimes another reader will find errors that you missed or identify areas that need revision. If your professor offers to read a first draft, always take him or her up on their offer, but only after you have spent time revising the paper on your own. The feedback they give you can be helpful in identifying if you have met their expectations.

Once you have revised your paper for content, format, grammar, and punctuation, you are ready to confidently submit the final draft. You will know you have put a significant amount of time in to preparing your assignment and that it is a display of your best work.

CHAPTER 5

Diversity

The college environment is rich with opportunities to meet and interact with a diverse array of students, faculty, and staff. As you begin your college journey, you have likely already started to experience many "firsts" with regard to your relationships with others: first time sharing a room; first time in a classroom with more than 30 students; first time working in a group with someone of a different race or culture. In many ways, college is unlike any other atmosphere you may have experienced. You not only share classrooms with students who may be unlike yourself, but you also live among one another and interact through your out-of-class activities. The next time you are walking through the student union or enjoying a meal with friends in your dining hall, look around and consider all of the people around you, sharing in a similar experience. You all have the common purpose of being in this same place, with the shared goal of making the most of your college experience, yet each of you brings a very unique perspective to the campus environment.

Drs. Randall and Katharine Hansen, founders of Quintessential Careers, reported that in addition to the skills necessary to complete a particular job, employers are seeking applicants who "demonstrate sensitivity and awareness to other people and cultures" (para 12). It is not enough to know how to do your job. Employers want to hire people who can also interact with a team. To be successful in the workplace, you must "have the ability to work with others in a professional manner while attempting to achieve a common goal" (para 15). College is a perfect environment to practice these skills and develop the important interpersonal competencies employers seek. The diversity of a college campus helps create a learning environment where you can think critically about important issues, develop and share strong opinions of your own, and consider the opinions of others.

The structure of a college campus as both a living and learning environment allows you to interact with people from diverse backgrounds in many different methods. You will meet different types of people everywhere you go on campus. You may have a roommate from another part of the United States or even from another country. Most likely, students in your classes will have varying and controversial opinions about current national and international issues. Though their views often will not align with your own, you can benefit from hearing their various points of view. For example, you may have non-traditional-aged students in some of your classes. These students will contribute unique perspectives to classroom discussions. Likewise, you may meet an international student while waiting in line for coffee or attending a campus event. You also may make friends of differing sexual orientations or your roommate may have a disability.

Additionally, a professor's ethnicity may differ substantially from yours. Everyone you meet during your college journey brings a wealth of unique life experiences, which will raise the quality of your in- and out-of-class discussions.

Expanding Your World View

Consider taking advantage of some of these activities to help you expand your view of the communities in which you live and learn:

- *Enroll in a course that looks at a race, religion, or gender different from your own.*
- *Interview a student who has studied abroad to find out about his/her experiences.*
- *Introduce yourself to international students in your classes. Like you, they may be new to campus and often are eager to meet American students.*
- *Ask a nontraditional-age student in your class to study or serve with you on a group project.*
- *Include a semester or summer of studying abroad in your academic plan.*
- *Seek out faculty and staff who have an academic interest in international issues and learn how they entered their field or discipline.*
- *Attend local festivals that are sponsored by international or religious organizations.*
- *Learn a second language.*
- *Read biographies of human rights and social activists.*
- *Read the newspaper regularly to stay current with local, national, and international issues.*

(CONT'D)

College life is about being comfortable with your views while also being open to living with and learning from others. We learn most from those whose experiences, beliefs, and perspectives are different from our own. Moreover, these lessons can be learned best in a richly diverse, intellectual, and social environment. Diversity on a college campus enriches your educational experiences. Education within a diverse setting, such as a college campus, prepares you to become a good citizen in an increasingly complex society. Diversity fosters mutual respect and teamwork. It also helps build communities whose members are judged by the quality of their character and contributions, not by their external appearance or other stereotypical beliefs.

Discovering Yourself

Before you can understand the perspectives of others, you must first understand your own ideas and recognize the situations and events that have shaped who you are today. The many experiences that you have had and the people who you have interacted with influence who you are. There are some events or relationships that we may easily recognize as having an impact on our views of others and ourselves. For example, the relationship you have with your parents or guardians has likely impacted the way you view many situations. The peers you spent time with in elementary and secondary school have affected what you expect of your friends in college. Your views toward social issues may have been shaped by your religious viewpoints or your experiences with injustice. You may be quite aware of some of the elements that have shaped who you are. However, there are probably other elements of your identity you are less likely to think about on a daily basis.

As you begin meeting new people and making new friends, you may start to recognize the impact your background and experiences have had on shaping the person you are. Your background has shaped your ideas, opinions, learning styles, beliefs, and values. The opportunity to share your background while exploring the lives of those around you can be one of the most meaningful learning experiences of your college career.

Consider the following questions and make note of what you might say if you were to meet someone new and they asked you:

- *What words would you use to describe yourself?*
- *Who are the people who have most influenced your life?*
- *What behaviors do you practice regularly that you think most exemplify who you are? (ex: enthusiastic student, church-goer, avid reader, athlete, singer, writer)*
- *What is it about those behaviors that inspire you to want to do well?*
- *What major events in your life have impacted how you think, act, and view the world?*
- *When you think of the life you have led up to this point, what accomplishments are you most proud of?*
- *When you are getting the most joy or pleasure out of life, what are you doing? Who are you with? How often do you take part in this type of experience?*

The answers to these questions will help lead you to a greater familiarity with your sense of self and identity. Developing your self-awareness does not happen overnight. We often don't realize how an event or individual has impacted our way of thinking until we begin to view our life as it relates to that of a new friend or peer. As you meet and interact with new people, you will not only increase your awareness of the unique traits of others but also your awareness of yourself.

Understanding Your Peers

When you hear the term "diversity," what comes to mind? Do you think of the many faces you walk past on your way to class each day? These faces likely include students who look much like you and those who may look very different from you. The diversity of your campus community is made up of many factors, including ethnicity, age, geographic

- *Take classes in a wide variety of subjects such as political science, humanities, women's studies, African-American studies, Latino and immigrant studies, or Chinese.*
- *Ask questions during class discussions if you do not understand the viewpoints of the professor, guest speaker, or another classmate.*
- *Attend organizational meetings that you usually would not attend.*
- *Volunteer to be a note-taker for a student with a learning disability.*

Stereotypes

A stereotype is an "image of or attitude toward persons or groups that is not based on observation and experience but on preconceived ideas or an artificial construction about that person or group" (Barfield, 1997). Consider the stereotypes students may face based on the broad assumptions that society makes about these groups:

- *Student Athletes*
- *Fraternity/Sorority Members*
- *Asian Students*
- *Gay, Lesbian, or Transgender Students*
- *Older Students*
- *Other:*

Consider a characteristic of yourself that carries a stereotype and make a list of the assumptions people may make about you based on that affiliation:

Because I am ....

people assume that I:

Stereotypes are not usually meant to hurt others. However, they can keep you from being able to get to know people for who they really are. Challenge yourself to abandon your assumptions about a group of students and get to know people who are unlike yourself. You may find that they don't meet any of the assumptions you had toward them. You may also have a good time laughing about the assumptions other people have made toward their group.

upbringing, economic background, academic ability, sexual orientation, and physical ability. You can likely identify many characteristics of your classmates and faculty that make your community diverse. However, the characteristics that contribute to the diverse makeup of your campus cannot be identified by physical appearance.

Multiculturalism is the practice of acknowledging and respecting the various cultures, religions, races, ethnicities, attitudes, and opinions within an environment. Recognizing the complexities of what individuals bring to your learning environment and developing an understanding and respect for your peers is part of the process of understanding multiculturalism. To practice the act of multiculturalism, you must first understand the components that make up the culture of individuals and groups of individuals. A word often confused with race is *ethnicity*. While race is commonly associated with the color of our skin, ethnicity is associated with the environment into which you are born. The term "ethnicity" can be used to further explain ourselves. For example, you recently completed your college applications, which likely asked you to select one of the following choices with which you would identify yourself: African-American/Black, Hispanic/Latino, Asian/Pacific Islander, Native American, or White/Non-Hispanic. These selections may appear simple, but there is much to consider before selecting an appropriate response. Ethnicity is a facet of diversity that encompasses a social subgroup's geographical location, assigned or assumed gender roles, choice of language, literature, music, history, religion, values, cultural norms, and other characteristics that give a group a unique identity. Some characteristics may be more prevalent in certain ethnicities or may be perceived as distinctive characteristics due to societal assumptions. For instance, two individuals may be identified by race as black, but separately represent such ethnicities as African-American and Jamaican. Both individuals may appear to be black, but their varying ethnicities indicate a more complex personal identification. Many white individuals do not consider their ethnicity as determining their identity. However, ethnicity is a key identifying characteristic for all individuals. For example, your race may be white, but your ethnicity could be Italian, Irish, German, or Polish.

Your ethnicity is likely to influence your *culture*. Culture is the "shared traditions, knowledge, beliefs, art, morals, law, customs, language, and rituals of a given human population group defined as sharing these elements" (Barfield, 1997). Consider some of your daily habits and annual traditions. Many cultural indicators such as food, music, and holiday celebrations vary based on ethnic norms. Depending on your ethnicity and cultural practices, you may do things similarly or differently from your peers. Remember that when we act and express ourselves, we reveal much of our varying cultural backgrounds.

Our culture is often shaped by our geographic location. We tend to eat food similar to that of our neighbors, and listen to music that is particular to our region. Our environment responds to that culture by providing services that are in demand from the citizens in the area. Therefore, students who attend a college far from home may experience "culture shock" as they begin to learn about their new environment. Consider the additional challenges that come with attending college in a new region:

- *Locating grocery stores or restaurants that offer the foods you enjoy.*
- *Learning the dialect or slang of the region.*
- *Identifying a church or place of worship that feels comfortable and inviting.*
- *Finding a salon or barber shop.*
- *Navigating a new public transportation system or coping with the lack of public transportation.*
- *Building relationships with faculty or mentors who understand your background as well as your future goals.*

If you are an in-state student or are familiar with the community near campus, you can assist your out-of-state peers by orienting them to the services near campus, offering to take them on a tour of the area, or inviting them to join you when you are taking advantage of some of the local services. You can learn a lot from someone who may share your race or ethnicity but has different

Leaving Your Legacy

As a nation, we have made great strides in recognizing one another's needs and our responsibility to care for one another. *We can find inspiration in the words of many great leaders who have worked to promote an understanding and appreciation of our differences.*

"I have a dream that my four little children will one day live in a nation where they will not be judged by the color of their skin, but by the content of their character."

– Martin Luther King, Jr. Civil Rights Activist

"We all live with the objective of being happy; our lives are all different and yet the same."

– Anne Frank, Jewish Holocaust victim, from a diary entry at age 14

"We have become not a melting pot but a beautiful mosaic. *Different people, different beliefs, different yearnings, different hopes, different dreams."*

– Jimmy Carter, 39th President of the United States of America

"I will never forget that the only reason I'm standing here today is because somebody, somewhere, stood up for me when it was risky. *Stood up when it was hard. Stood up when it wasn't popular. And because that somebody stood up, a few more stood up. And then a few thousand stood up. And then a few million stood up. And standing up, with courage and clear purpose, they somehow managed to change the world."*

– Barack Obama, 44th President of the United States of America

(CONT'D)

cultural perspectives. You may inspire one another to explore new things like food, music, dancing styles, and languages.

Discovering Your Community

As you become more comfortable with your own self-awareness and begin to understand the various cultures of your peers, you can further expand your multiculturalism by exploring the communities in which you live. You are a member of many communities. If you live on campus, you belong to a community of hall mates; each of your classes is a community of learners with a shared interest in the presented material; you belong to a community of scholars within your major or course of study. You are part of the many facets of your campus, local, state, national and international communities, and as such have an obligation to give back to the communities that have given you the opportunity to learn and grow.

The college environment is rich with opportunities to engage in your community through service. When you are motivated to serve others, it is often an external emotion, the desire to help others that prompts you to act. However, you can reap many benefits and develop meaningful skills through participating in community service.

BENEFITS OF COMMUNITY SERVICE

There is a wealth of research that has explored the outcomes students experience as a result of engaging in their community through volunteering. When you commit to serving others, you will find many benefits for yourself as well.

- ***Exposure to Diversity, Multiculturalism, and Different Ways of Thinking.*** *By becoming involved in various aspects of community life, students gain new information to consider and new ways to think about things. Frequently, students "learn a lot from conversing with those whom they help or work with, as they may encounter new points of view." (LeSourd, 1997)*
- ***Overall Wellness.*** *Students who volunteer report lower levels of stress, positive feelings about themselves, and increased satisfaction with life. (Thoits & Hewitt, 2001)*

- ***It Feels Good!*** *The number-one reason young people name for volunteering is that it makes them feel good! (Current Health 1, 1998)*
- ***Making Friends.*** *Participation in service activities affords you an opportunity to meet friends outside the classroom or residence hall environments.*
- ***Feelings of Trust, Cooperation, and Citizenship.*** *Volunteering can create positive feelings that "increase trust and cooperation—that can then promote greater political involvement in public affairs." (Smith, 1999)*
- ***Critical-Thinking and Problem-Solving Skills.*** *Through volunteering, you have the opportunity to make decisions about issues that interest and are important to you. When you think more deeply about the issue you are working with, you practice more complex thinking skills. (Hedin, 1989)*
- ***Improved Communication Skills.*** *Volunteering allows you to practice your communication skills with a variety of audiences using a variety of methods.*
- ***Increased Understanding of the Community or Issue.*** *You learn more when you have the opportunity to apply your knowledge to real-life situations. By volunteering, you can apply what you learn in the classroom with what you practice in the community.*
- ***Political and Civic Awareness.*** *"Through participation in voluntary associations, students develop a keener appreciation for civic affairs and understand more completely their obligations to participate in the political process." (Smith, 1999)*
- ***You'll Want to Come Back for More!*** *Students who participate in service feel an increased desire to help others and are likely to make volunteering a priority in their life.*

"If you don't understand yourself you don't understand anybody else."
– Nikki Giovanni, African-American poet

When she reflected on her experience at the University of Maryland, Katayoun Deljoui, a 2004 graduate, shared this reflection in her commencement speech: "…college is where I learned that America is not a melting pot. *By calling the United States a melting pot, people imply that all the ingredients must mix together and thus lose all distinction to become a new entity. I think America is a salad bowl. The ingredients many with different flavors and colors are combined, but they remain distinct. Only the dressing of freedom and tolerance holds them together."*

What legacy will you leave on your campus?

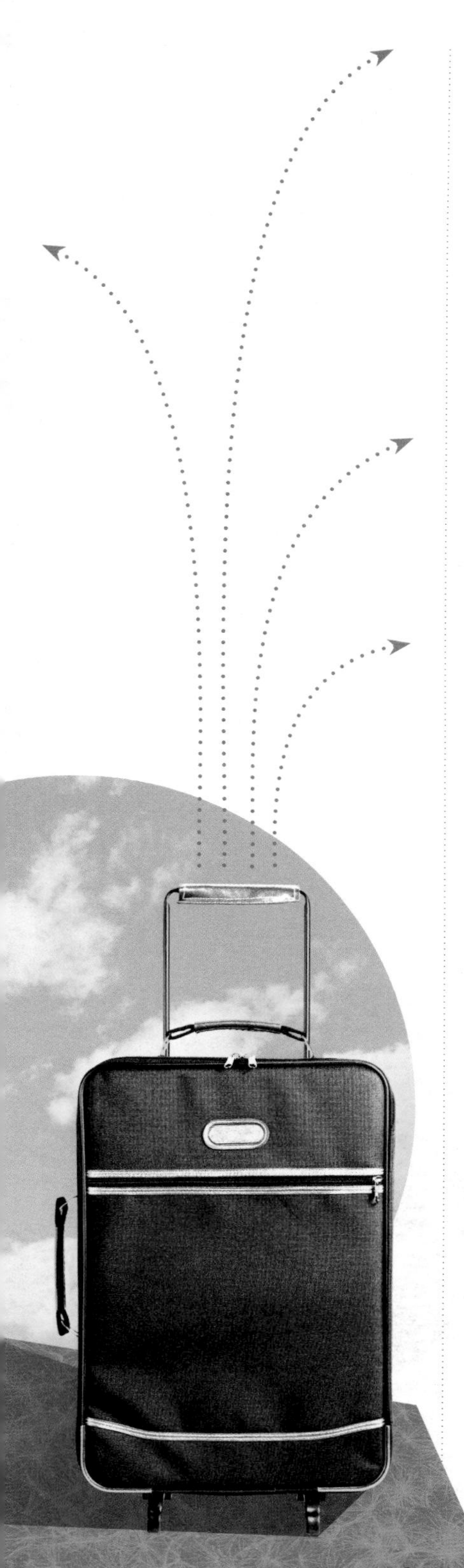

Recently, natural disasters such as Hurricane Katrina and the earthquake devastation in Haiti have prompted many college students to take action. Students have been motivated to help others and explore new places through alternative break trips, such as spring break, to help restore areas that have been affected by disaster, and by fundraising through a variety of efforts including concerts, T-shirt sales, telethons, blood donation drives, and food and clothing collections. These efforts are impressive and admirable, but it doesn't take a natural disaster to inspire a sense of service. You can make a difference in the lives of others by performing service in a variety of ways. Find something you are passionate about, a cause that you believe in, or a group that you identify needs help, and get to work! You may volunteer as a dog walker at a local pet shelter, organize a trash pickup on campus or in a nearby park, spend a Saturday helping to organize the pantry at a local food bank, or serving a meal at the Salvation Army. You will find that by working to help others, you learn a lot about yourself!

Discovering Your World

Studying abroad can be the adventure of a lifetime! By studying in a foreign country, you will have the opportunity to discover a new culture, practice a different language, learn independence as you travel to new and exciting places, and meet people from all over the world—all while receiving graduation credits!

The benefits of studying abroad are similar to those that you receive from providing service to a community. Students who study abroad report that they felt the experience helped them to become more mature and self-confident while also increasing their tolerance and understanding of others. Study-abroad participants also report that, as a result of their experience, they were more likely to seek out diverse friends when they returned to campus (Dwyer & Peters, 2004).

We're all deeply influenced by our surroundings. The thing is, we never realize this until we step out of them. Studying abroad is probably the single best way to step outside what you know and to discover the wider world. It's often difficult—you'll probably find that you have to question many of your beliefs about yourself, your country, your goals, etc. But ultimately, it's very rewarding! When you return from studying abroad, you're likely to have developed a better sense of who you are and what you want to do in life.

Some tips for a successful study-abroad experience:

- *Try to immerse yourself in the language and culture of the country as much as possible. Try not to live with other Americans, and make special efforts to befriend people in your host country (it's often easiest just to make friends with other exchange students).*
- *Unless you have a good reason for doing it, don't study in an English-speaking country. A big part of studying abroad is to learn a new language and push yourself to think in terms you're not used to. Foreign languages are a big part of this!*
- *Get to know your host country well. Particularly if you're in Europe—you'll be tempted to travel to nearby countries, and you should. But make sure you take the time to get to know your own host country. Take hikes in the countryside, buy food in local markets, and read local newspapers.*

Conclusion

Throughout your college career, actively seek opportunities to learn more about the people with whom you live, learn, and interact—both on campus and in the surrounding community. There are many areas of diversity to explore during your college years. Opportunities abound to learn about other cultures, observe how others behave, and, most importantly, learn more about yourself. Already, you have taken on the challenge to better yourself by continuing your education at the college level. Continue to challenge yourself with new experiences and opportunities so you will develop an unwavering respect for and understanding of diversity. By doing so, you will become a better student and more informed citizen.

Nondominant Hand Exercise

If you are an American student, it can be difficult to imagine what it's like to come to a new country and try to learn the language, culture, and behaviors of your peers. If you have the opportunity to meet and befriend an international student, they may offer some insight as to how his or her transition to college differs from yours, but also how the assimilation to your campus culture has been similar to yours.

A fun way to simulate what it might be like to have to learn a new way of doing things is to practice writing with your nondominant hand.

Using the hand you do not normally write with:

Write this sentence: I am writing this with my nondominant hand.

Sign your name:

Draw a square:

Draw a tree:

Write today's date:

Consider what it felt like to have to perform a normal task in an abnormal way.

What did you have to do differently in order to accomplish the task?

If you were required to write with your nondominant hand most of the time for the next two to four years, what do you think would happen?

Once proficient with your nondominant hand would you have lost the ability to write with your dominant hand?

How do you think this experience relates to the experience of moving to a new culture?

References

Barfield, T (Ed). (1997). *The dictionary of anthropology.* Blackwell Publishers.

Brewster, M., Gillespie, J.S., Burke, J., Hilt, S., Megyeri, K., Jokela, M., Whittle, D.D. (1991). *The English journal.* 80(6), 89-91.

Current Health 1. (1998). Helping others is good for you. *Current Health 1.* 22(2), 21-23.

Dwyer, M.M., Peters, C.K. (2004). The benefits of study abroad: New study confirms significant gains. *Transitions Abroad*, 37(5), 56.

Hansen, R.S., & Hansen, K. (2010). What do employers really want? Top skills and values employers seek from job-seekers. Retrieved from: http://www.quintcareers.com/job_skills_values.html

LeSourd, Sandra J. (1997). Community service in a multicultural nation. *Theory into practice.* 36(3),157-163.

Smith, S.R. (1999). Comment: Volunteering and community service. Law and contemporary problems, 62(4). *Amateurs in public service: Volunteering, service-learning, and community service,* 169-176.

Thoits, P.A., & Hewitt, L.N. (2001). Volunteer work and well-being. *Journal of health and social behavior,* 42(2),115-131.

University of Michigan. Benefits of student participation in community service. How does helping others help students? Web article retrieved from: http://sitemaker.umich.edu/356.black/home

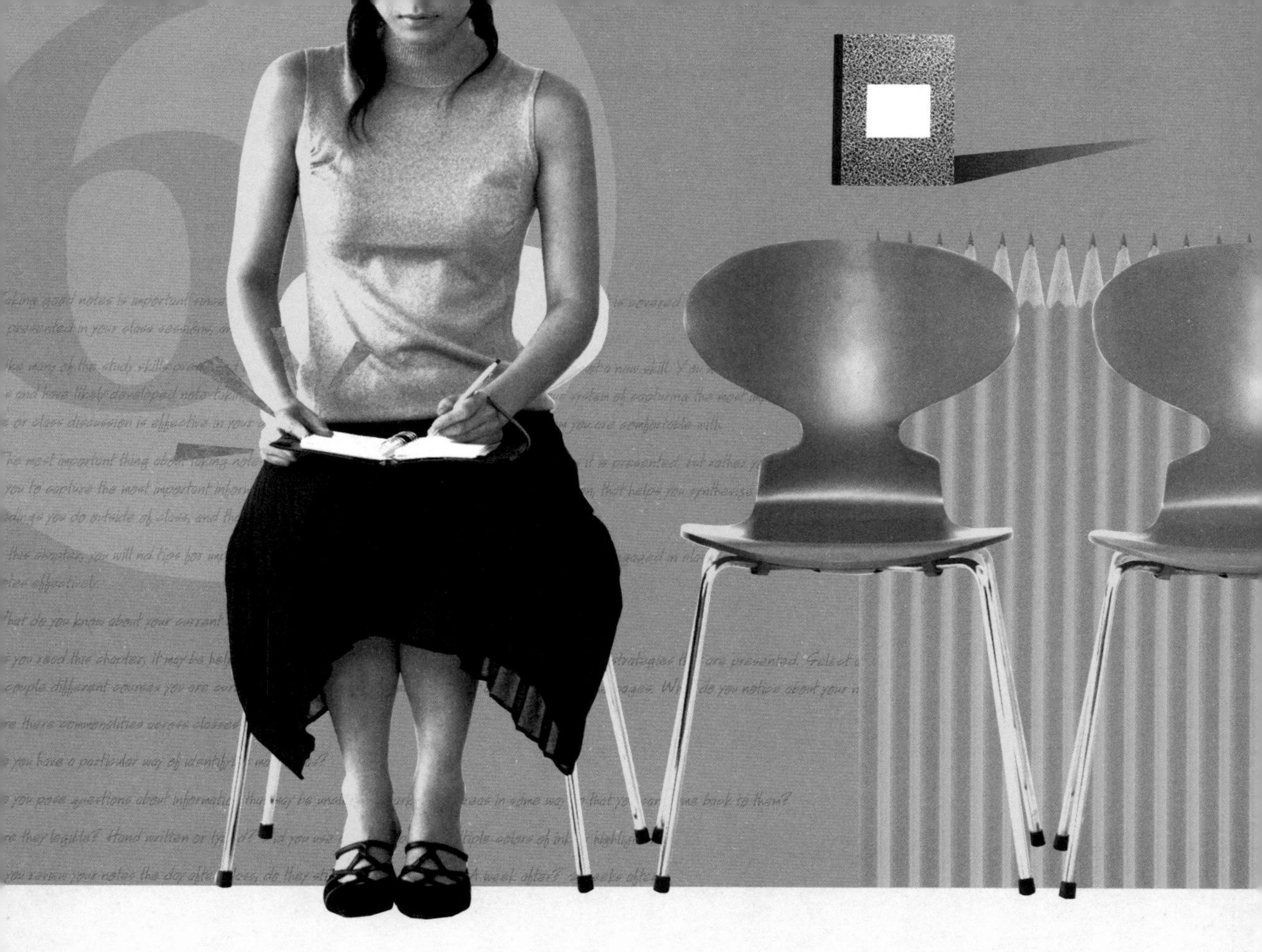

CHAPTER 6

Taking Notes

Taking good notes is important as most professors' exams include information that is covered in class.

You most likely will not remember everything that is presented in your class sessions, and taking notes helps you to recall important concepts. Like many of the study skills presented in this book, taking notes is not a new skill.

You were expected to take notes in your high school classes and have likely developed note-taking strategies that work for you. You may find that your system of capturing the most important information that is presented in a lecture or class discussion is effective in your college courses. If so, continue to use the system you are comfortable with. The most important thing about taking notes is not to follow a particular system exactly as it is presented, but rather to find a system that works for you—one that allows you to capture the most important information and helps you synthesize the information that is shared in class with the readings you do outside of class, and that helps you effectively prepare for exams and assignments. In this chapter, you will find tips for improving your note-taking skills, including strategies for staying engaged in class lectures, organizing your information, and using your notes effectively.

What Do You Know About Your Current Note-Taking Strategy?

As you read this chapter, it may be helpful to have a few sets of notes to review as you consider the strategies that are presented. Select a few sets of in-class notes from a couple different courses you are currently enrolled in and review the format and structure of the pages. What do you notice about your notes?

- *Are there commonalities across classes?*
- *Do you have a particular way of identifying main ideas?*
- *Do you pose questions about information that may be unclear or mark these areas in some way so that you can come back to them?*
- *Are they legible? Hand-written or typed? Did you use pencil or pen? Multiple colors of ink or highlighters?*
- *If you review your notes the day after class, do they still make sense to you? A week after? Two weeks after?*

TIPS for Effective Note-Taking

Ditch the cheap seats. *Grab a spot at the front of the room, toward the center of the row, to minimize distractions and maximize your view of the board and the professor.*

Be an active listener. *Bring your reading notes and any questions you have to class; make connections between your readings and class lectures; and consider the relevance of the information being presented by applying it to your life.*

Listen for clues to test items. *You can pick up on the change in an instructor's voice and pace when he or she is saying something that is important. Be sure to identify in your notes the ideas the professor focused on or repeated, and revisit that material during test preparation.*

Use short phrases, not full sentences. *Identify abbreviations that work for you and use those to save time and space.*

Be neat and organized. *Start a new page for each class session. Include at the top of each section the date and topic of the class discussion. Also, leave blank space between major topics so that you can fill in additional information later.*

Capture ideas as well as facts. *Don't only listen for dates and places—also make note of the ideas that help bring relevance to the information.*

(CONT'D)

The Art of Listening

Now that you have spent some time observing your current note-taking skills, you can identify areas where you can improve to make your class notes a more effective study tool. The key to good note-taking is good listening. It may be difficult to stay focused on a lecture if you are not interested in the content. Taking notes gives you something to focus on and can help you stay engaged with what is happening in class. You may have found, or may find in the future, that you have trouble keeping up with an instructor or following along with his or her lecture style. Perhaps the professor speaks quickly, and while you are writing one idea, you miss the next important concept. Sometimes the opposite occurs and the pace of the class is slow, and therefore you find yourself becoming distracted, losing interest, or daydreaming. Being an engaged listener can be challenging, but there are behaviors that can help you stay alert, even during your least favorite course.

You are more likely to listen to information that you are interested in. When you review your sample of notes, you probably see that you take the best notes for the classes that you are most interested in. This is because you are able to stay more engaged in the class discussions and are more comfortable with the material. It is especially important, therefore, that you practice active listening in the courses that you find less interesting. Being an active listener starts before the class begins. Having a positive frame of mind can help you succeed. If physics is your least favorite course, you may find yourself dreading going to class. Recognize that your attitude about this course is negative, and set small goals to help you stay motivated. For example, "If I stay alert and focused in physics today, I will treat myself to a frozen coffee at the bookstore after class." You can set yourself up for success with a positive attitude, and a front-row seat. Studies have shown that students who sit in the front and center of a classroom receive better grades than students who sit in the back. Everyone paid the same price for the class, why not take the best seat in the house? Sitting up front helps eliminate distractions and also keeps you closer to the instructor so that you can hear clearly and be less tempted to daydream.

Once you are comfortably seated, be prepared to take notes from the start of the class. Often the first few minutes of a lecture can give you clues about the most important information. If the professor lists the goals he or she wants to accomplish for the class session, write those down and organize your notes using the session goals as your main ideas. When you are listening to the lecture, pay attention for phrases such as "most significant" or "the most important" that may signify a key concept. Active listeners will also pick up on inflection or emphasis in the professor's voice that may indicate an important idea. If the professor pauses to allow the class time to write, it is because he or she wants to be sure you get the information into your notes. It is important that you don't try to write down every word that a professor says but that you listen for the most important information.

An active listener is a busy listener. Having something to do can help you stay focused, especially if you find yourself losing interest in a topic. One way to stay attentive during class is to create an assignment for yourself. As you are completing your course readings, identify questions you have about the material. Bring those questions with you to class and listen for the answers during the class lecture or discussion. If you don't find the answers, ask the professor—he or she will be impressed that you are making connections between the course readings and the class session. Some professors will post class notes prior to the class session. Bring a printout of those notes with you and use them as a guide. Do not make the mistake of using the provided slides or notes as a substitute for attending class or taking your own notes. Notes that are provided by the professor are meant to help you identify the most important ideas, but you will be tested on the provided notes as well as the lecture material. If a professor takes the time to write something on the board, it is probably important. He or she may also present information using a picture or diagram. This can help you to understand how concepts are connected so try to illustrate the diagram in your own notes, using labels and key words that you will remember later.

Compare your notes with a partner. *It is a good idea to compare notes with a classmate to identify any information you may have missed but he or she got, and vice versa.*

Revisit your notes, regularly. *Refer to your class notes each day to ensure that you are committing the information to memory (see memory curve information on page 24 in the Reading chapter). Clear up any discrepancies or gaps in your notes by following up with the professor at the next class session.*

Study with notes from various sources. *When you begin studying for an exam, it is important that you refer to your notes not only from class lectures but also from your reading and any supplemental course materials. Professors will expect you to be familiar with information from all of your course resources.*

Another active-listening strategy is to take the information and begin to commit it to your memory. If the professor provides an example through the use of a story or real application, take a few notes about the story. This can help you remember the concept when you review your notes after class. If the professor does not provide examples, think of your own applications for the material. It is easier to remember information if you see the relevance to your own life.

Effective note-taking does not consist of transcribing the lecture but rather identifying the key points, making note of the most important ideas, and noting the concepts that may have been unclear so that you can return to them after class and clarify any information you may have misunderstood. As you attend more classes with a professor, you will learn his or her presentation style and it will become easier to take effective notes.

Note-Taking Models

The Reading Skills chapter introduced you to the mapping method of note-taking (see page 23). Mapping main ideas to supporting ideas is also an effective way to organize your in-class notes. It may be difficult to map the professor's ideas during class. But when you revisit your notes after class, you can organize the material and connect the key concepts by mapping the information and then combining it with the notes you took from the course readings. If the mapping strategy has been an effective way for you to organize your reading notes, you may consider using it for the notes you take in class.

CORNELL METHOD

The Cornell method of note-taking is centered on the idea that your paper is divided into various segments, helping you to organize the material in a systematic way. When practicing the Cornell method, you use a larger left margin, about two inches, and reserve that space to record your "cues" or topic headings that will alert you to the information that is contained in that area of your notes. Use the remainder of the page to take the majority of your notes, making sure to skip a few lines between each major idea and concept. This method can be helpful when you review your notes to determine if you have mastered the material. You should be able to cover the right side of your page where the majority of the information is contained and go down the left side calling out the cues. If you can explain each cue without looking at the notes in the area to the right, you have effectively recalled the information.

Practice the Cornell method with the notes that you collected from your classes. Using the sample layout below, transfer your notes into the Cornell format. You may find that this type of organization helps you to more easily identify the key information that you need to recall.

Use this section for key words, questions, etc.

Take notes here during class.

Write a summary of your notes here.

THE SENTENCE METHOD

In the sentence method of note-taking, notes pages are organized line by line, with each new fact or topic on a separate line. This can be especially effective if you have an instructor who provides a lot of facts or details through a fast-paced lecture. This method allows you to capture the facts quickly, leaving space to go back later and make connections between ideas. An example of recording information using the sentence method:

> *The professor says: "The University was founded in 1864 as a result of the Morrill Act of 1862. This act allowed federal land to be given to states to be used for the development of college and universities that would offer science, engineering, and agricultural studies. Pages 134-138 further explain the details of the Morrill Act and the institutions that resulted from this movement."*

You would record:

Morrill Act-federal grant for development of colleges to offer sci., engnr., and ag. See text pp. 134-138.

The sentence method helps to keep your information organized in the order it is presented by the professor. However, if the lecturer does not provide information in an organized fashion, it may be difficult to cluster related ideas without having to rewrite the notes. Students who use the sentence method often type their notes as a way of reviewing, making it easier to move sentences around and group similar ideas.

THE OUTLINING METHOD

You are likely familiar with the process of outlining information, using a number and letter system to organize ideas and concepts. The practice of outlining can also be used as a note-taking strategy. The outlining method encourages note takers to start each major idea to the left of the page, indenting below that point for the facts that support the idea. Details of the facts are further indented and so on and so on.

I. XYZ University-Founded 1864
    a. Morrill Act-1862
    (See pages 134-138)
        i. Federal land given to states
        ii. Sci., engr., ag programs

Outlining is a skill that is introduced early in secondary education. Therefore, most students are comfortable with the format and understand the process of organizing information this way. Do you see any evidence of outlining in your sample notes? Are you able to identify what topics would be the main ideas and what supporting information would come below those ideas? Practice organizing your notes using the outlining method.

I. Major Idea
    a. Supporting Fact
    b. Supporting Fact
        i. Detail
        ii. Detail

II. Major Idea #2
    a. Supporting Fact
        i. Detail
    b. Supporting Fact

Conclusion

Mastering the skill of note-taking requires practice and flexibility. You will likely find that you have to adapt the way you take notes depending on the structure and content of your course. For example, you may prefer the sentence method for a history class when the professor is presenting information in a chronological format, making notes of many dates and locations. However, the sentence method may be difficult to use with math or science classes where many of the notes are presented as formulas or equations. Likewise, you may prefer the Cornell method for taking notes from an organized class lecture, but find the process of mapping to be better suited for your discussion-based seminar courses. The key to effective note-taking is to identify what works best for you! When your notes are organized and accurate, they can serve as an effective tool to help you learn the information that is presented through in- and out-of-class activities and assignments.

CHAPTER 7

Developing Critical-Thinking Skills

What does critical thinking mean to me?

Perhaps Socrates encouraged the emergence of the concept of thinking critically—both in academic settings and life experiences—when he stated, "An unexamined life is not worth living."

Increasingly, students, as well as instructors and faculty, are becoming aware that the college/university experience triggers a life-long habit of thinking critically. It is important that students become good and proactive critics of their own thinking and learning.

Learning to think critically is an ongoing and unending process. It impacts how you, as a student, approach college, your readings, your work, and assignments. Thinking critically is a skill set you need to begin cultivating, practicing, and refining on a daily basis.

More and more, employers in the "new economy" are looking for employees who can think critically and problem-solve in the workplace. These skills, along with teamwork, collaboration, and communication skills, are important and valued. The ability to think critically across subjects and situations is important, no matter what your discipline or major. It is worth your time and effort to take the subject of developing critical-thinking skills seriously. Spend time carefully reading and studying the information in this section. Be sure to thoughtfully and completely address the application components of this section.

Critical thinking was defined in 1987 by Michael Scriven and Richard Paul at the 8th International Conference on Critical Thinking and Education Reform as:

> *"Critical thinking is the intellectually disciplined process of actively and skillfully conceptualizing, applying, analyzing, synthesizing, and/or evaluating information gathered from, or generated by, observation, experience, reflection, reasoning, or communication, as a guide to belief and action.*
> *In its exemplary form, it is based on universal intellectual values that transcend subject matter divisions: clarity, accuracy, precision, consistency, relevance, sound evidence, good reasons, depth, breadth, and fairness...."*

This definition involves many parts and concepts. It is important to understand its meaning.

In the form provided below, write down each of the key words in this definition.

Choose ten words from the definition. Look up each word or concept in a reliable source or dictionary and write its meaning. Think about the meaning of each word and whether or not you practice these concepts in your thinking. For example, do you actively and skillfully conceptualize and apply information that you read and learn about from your classes?

Following the definitions of each of the ten words, discuss your areas of strength and weakness based on this definition of critical thinking with at least one peer. Then write what the practice of thinking critically means to you in your college experience. Be specific; think carefully about your response.

Word 1:

Word 2:

Word 3:

Word 4:

Word 5:

Word 6:

Word 7:

Word 8:

Word 9:

Word 10:

What critical thinking means to me in my college experience:

Critical Thinking: Best Practices for Students

It is important to strategize how you can incorporate critical thinking on a daily basis in each subject you are studying. Think about critical questions and concepts when reading and studying course material. Also, think about identifying these critical questions and concepts when engaging in classwork and activities. As you work to become a better critical thinker you will begin to identify challenges or problems related to the critical content of the course in a focused way, and be able to state the issues succinctly and clearly. Know and state the key parts of related challenges or questions. Write out the key questions along with related challenges and questions in 1-2 sentences for each key concept and related question/challenge.

Then begin to gather information and facts relevant to the question or challenge. Gather this information in an unbiased fashion, remaining open to any facts or opinions. Organize the information in a logical fashion, including that with which you agree and disagree. Proceed to logically consider all information and points of view in an unbiased manner. Use this information to make your best predictions or judgments related to the problem or challenge. Analyze the assumptions underlying your thinking. Are they clear and unbiased? Did you consider differing points of view? Are your underlying assumptions reasonable?

Develop your rationale in a clear and fair manner. State your thinking and conclusions clearly and in an unbiased fashion. Think about the implications from various points of view and angles. Reasonably consider your predictions. Ask others who you trust and who have experience with this problem/ challenge for their feedback and suggestions. How would they view this problem or challenge differently? Consider sharing your thoughts and opinions with those who are more experienced critical thinkers. Develop and state your opinions and conclusions, based on the process above. Start immediately and refine this practice of thinking critically on a daily basis. Make it a habit to approach your studies in this manner. Make it a personal goal to think more critically about all material that you read and study for your classes.

Listen and think critically to your professor as well as to your peers. Work toward developing critical-thinking skills for life-long practice. Be an active, engaged, critical thinker in every part of your college life and work.

As you study for your classes and participate in class discussions, as well as campus activities, consider adding the following practices to your study and personal habits:

1. ***Keep notes for each course of critical questions and problems.*** *Listen carefully in class for such critical questions and problems. As you are reading course material, actively think about questions, problems, and challenges raised in the material.*
2. ***Be an active, not passive, learner.*** *Be proactive in your learning. Always engage the content of your studies. Read and study all course material and come to class prepared, having carefully thought about the content of the readings.*
3. ***For each major reading section you study, prepare at least 3-4 questions or problem statements related to the content.*** *Think carefully about the material you are reading and studying. What questions do you have related to the course information? What areas pique your interest?*
4. ***Discuss your questions and problem statements with at least one peer.*** *Engage in an active discussion to consider possible responses to your questions/problems presented as a result of carefully considering the content you are studying.*

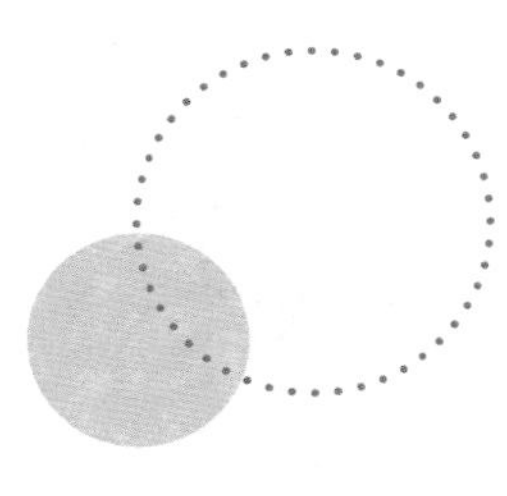

5. ***Select a few questions/problem statements that confuse you, or to which you remain unclear about an appropriate response/answer.*** *Talk with your professor about these selective questions. Be prepared and think carefully about how to summarize your own efforts to address these problems and questions.*
6. ***Reflect regularly.*** *Take time to be quiet and think for uninterrupted periods of time about the critical questions and challenges. Too many distractions interfere with clear, concise reflection and thinking. Find a quiet place for this activity.*
7. ***Always be looking for and tracking critical elements or important concepts of the material you are studying.*** *This information might also be called the "big ideas". Find a way to record and organize these major concepts for each course. Along with each big idea or concept, think about and record questions or problems related to this subject.*
8. ***Make webs and diagrams showing connections of course material you are learning.*** *Think carefully about and seek out the connections between the content studied within a course as well as outside the course. Make drawings and notes to show the connections or potential connections of your learning.*
9. ***Write out the big ideas or critical/major elements of material you are studying.*** *Following this listing, identify connections to real-world experiences, both in the present and in the future. Making connections to other learning experiences is important.*
10. ***Prior to each class, write out the big ideas from your advanced reading and study.*** *Along with each big idea, write 3-5 questions or problems you wish to think about that relate to the content of the big idea.*

11. ***Find study partners who are engaged and motivated to become better students.*** *Make time to reflect on the course material and big ideas with classmates. Think carefully about course material; ask each other challenging and probing questions and discuss problems presented by the material.*

12. ***Take an opposing position, as you might in a debate setting.*** *Think about the topic you are studying from as many angles or positions as possible. Play "devil's advocate" with course material. Is an opposing point of view possible or reasonable?*

13. ***For each major concept of a chapter reading, what is the most compelling and complex question or problem?*** *What interests you that is not immediately apparent? Keep a record of these compelling questions or problems. Bring your list to class. Think about these questions over the course of several days. Revisit your questions regularly. Write down your thoughts and responses.*

14. ***Use the technique of task-analysis.*** *If you are thinking about how to solve a challenge or problem, write down every step in order. Go back through your list and look for smaller steps or increments to solve your dilemma. This can prove helpful in thinking about how to tackle a challenge or problem.*

15. ***Work with another student or peer in the task-analysis process.*** *Do the process independently, and then compare notes. Contrast and compare your thoughts/steps/strategies. Discuss your relative approaches. Think about new ways, steps, and strategies to approach a challenge or problem.*

16. ***Seek the counsel of peers and students who are at a more advanced level within your subject or discipline.*** *Prior to discussing identified challenges or problems in your field of study, ask for their guidance and opinions. Learn from their advanced knowledge and prior thinking in the field of study. Carefully consider their comments and points of view. Record their thoughts and suggestions. Be a willing learner from others who are more experienced.*

17. ***Interact with people who are not like you—of different backgrounds and experiences.*** *Seek out the counsel of other students that you would not typically consider within your "circle" of friends. Ask for their opinions and why they have this opinion related to questions and challenges you pose to them. Be patient and always respectful of their responses. Carefully consider points of view you have not previously considered.*

18. ***Seek out students who have differing cultural experiences from yours.*** *Get to know international students. Ask about clubs or organizations on campus that cater to international students. Find out what these individuals think related to problems and challenges that you pose to them. Contrast with your own views. Make new connections in your thinking based on their thinking. Ask them about their value system and how it was developed. Get out of your comfort zone and learn from others who have had diverse life and cultural experiences. Value this information and use it to refine and to shape your own opinions to problems and challenges.*

19. ***Travel in areas where you are unfamiliar with the culture.*** *Ask questions in a respectful manner. Find out through your travel experiences how others who have differing cultural backgrounds view life differently. Compare and contrast to your own experiences. Try not to be judgmental in any way. Consider all opinions equally and fairly. Learn from differences to enhance your life.*

20. ***Prioritize the development of your critical-thinking skills.*** *Care about your progress in this important area. Reflect on your personal development of critical-thinking skills. Take charge and responsibility for the development of your critical-thinking skills. You alone are responsible and accountable to yourself for the careful and thoughtful development of your thinking capabilities.*

Review the 20 suggestions above that assist you in developing your critical-thinking skills. Go back through the list above and highlight those suggestions which are the most important for you to implement and work on during the next few weeks. From this list, select five priorities. List the five priorities on the next page, along with Actions to Take to implement the priorities.

Keep this list handy and use it to start refining and developing your critical-thinking skills in every facet of your college experience. You will benefit from the development of your critical-thinking skills in both your academic work and other areas of your life.

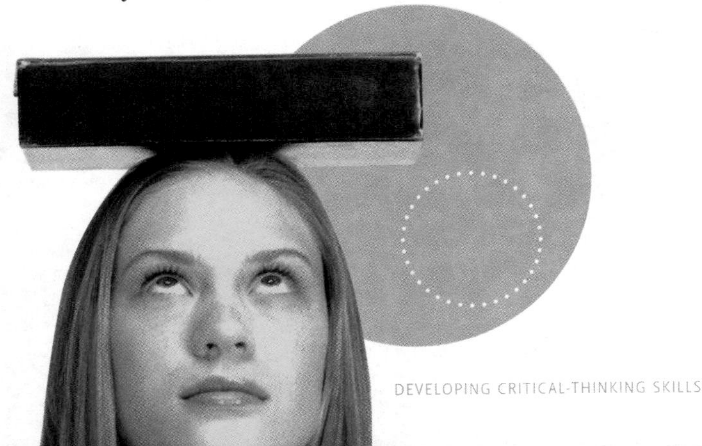

Priorities	Actions to Take/Implement
1	
2	
3	
4	
5	

CHAPTER 8

Studying for & Taking Tests

Testing is one of the most common methods college professors use to determine if students understand course content.

In most of your classes, you likely have exams of some type, either periodic tests, scheduled and unscheduled quizzes, or more significant and perhaps comprehensive midterm and final exams.

Whether you are a good test-taker or have difficulty preparing for and performing on tests, exams will be a major component of your grade in many courses. It is important that you identify preparation and test-taking strategies that work for you.

Practicing Effective Testing: Before, During, and After the Exam

BEFORE THE EXAM

High performance on an exam requires intentional preparation and attention leading up to the test, during the test, and following the test. A high-quality performance on an exam begins with effective preparation. You likely have some test-preparation strategies that you utilize already. Perhaps you are diligent about keeping up with class readings, or you review your notes each day. You may have a study or tutoring group that you meet with between tests to ensure you thoroughly understand the material. All of these proactive behaviors will assist you as you prepare for exam day.

Before you start practicing new strategies, identify practices you already have in your study skills set.

My three most effective strategies to prepare for an exam are:

1. ....

2. ....

3. ....

As you become more experienced with college-level examinations, you may find that your current strategies need to be supplemented with additional preparation behaviors. Cramming for an exam one or two days before the test period is not an effective way to comprehend information. If your most effective strategy is cramming, you will cause undue stress on yourself and likely forget the information shortly after the exam period.

Before you prepare for an exam or quiz, it is helpful to know the format that will be used to test your knowledge. Listen to cues during class sessions leading up to your test that may indicate the types of questions the professor will ask. If the instructor doesn't indicate the types of questions, ask about them! Most professors will share with students whether the exam will be multiple choice, true/false, or essay, as well as the point value of each item. This information will help you determine the best way to prepare. As you begin to prepare for the exam, you may also want to consult your course syllabus to determine what percentage of your grade in the course will be determined by the test. Knowing this type of information will lessen your anxiety as you approach the testing period.

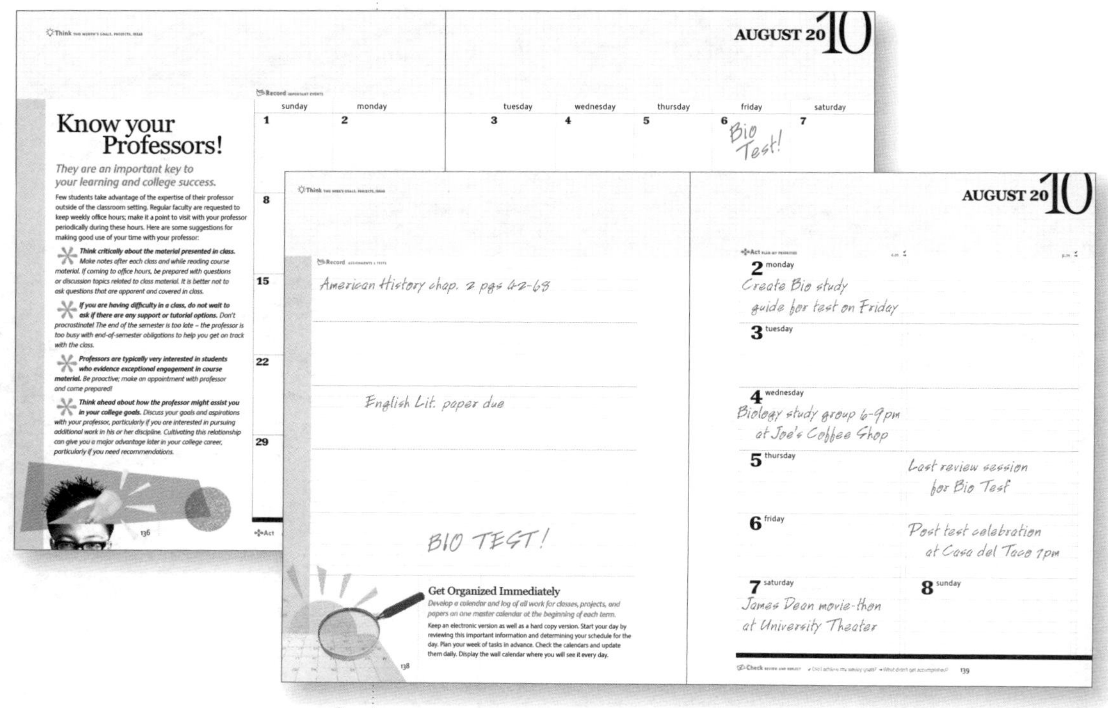

In the weeks leading up to a test you may have to adjust your normal study schedule to allow for some extra time to prepare. Identify the amount of time you can spend studying in one setting. If your attention begins to stray after 30 minutes, identify four to five 30-minute stretches throughout the week that you can use to review a small portion of the material. You may find that you can study for longer stretches of time like a full hour or 90 minutes. If you devote longer spans of time to one subject, remember to take short breaks every 30 minutes to help keep your focus on the material. If you are studying in the library, take a 10-minute walk around the floor or to the computer lab to check your e-mail. If you are studying in your room, grab a quick snack or go outside and take a short walk around the courtyard. Remember to limit your breaks to 10 minutes and quickly return to your studying. You will find that your mind is refreshed and able to take in information much more easily if you are rewarding yourself with scheduled breaks.

BRINGING IT ALL TOGETHER: Using Notes, Readings, and Study Guides to Prepare for an Exam

In previous chapters you were introduced to the SQ3R and mapping methods for critical reading, as well as a few note-taking strategies to assist you in fully understanding the information presented in your courses. If you use these strategies throughout the semester, you will be well prepared for any tests or quizzes. You may still find yourself feeling a bit panicked as the test date approaches, and that is a normal behavior. A certain level of anxiety can actually help you stay motivated to prepare for your test. As you review the information you will be tested on, be sure that you are not just reading the material over and over but are intentionally reviewing information you have already read, synthesizing that information with your class notes and handouts, and identifying through your preferred note-taking method the key concepts and topics. Once you feel you have mastered a concept, try to summarize the material or explain it to a friend. If you are able to accurately explain what you have reviewed, you are ready to move on to the next topic. As you move from one concept to the next, you should find yourself connecting the information you reviewed from previous sections to the

Test Prep Tips

- *Ask the professor what will be expected on the exam (concepts covered; types of questions; amount of time allowed).*
- *Schedule extra study time in the weeks leading up to your test during the time of day when you are most alert. Remember to reward yourself with short breaks during long study sessions.*
- *When you have multiple tests on the same day or in the same week, study your weakest subjects first while your energy is high and you have a more keen focus.*
- *Visit your professor to discuss any questions you have about material that may be included on the test—don't be afraid to ask your professor for help.*
- *Create sample tests using the format that the professor indicated (essay, multiple choice, matching) and use these as practice for the real test.*
- *If you find that studying with a group is helpful for you, ask two to three classmates to meet for a preparation session. Have each member create a few test questions on an assigned topic and combine them to create practice tests. Have everyone take the practice tests independently and discuss any discrepancies in your answers.*

(CONT'D)

material you are currently reviewing.

You may find that you have multiple tests in a week or within a short period of time. Do not panic! You may have to alter your normal test preparation schedule so you can fit in an ample amount of study time for all of your tests. However, if you are practicing on-going preparation, you should not need to pull any "all nighters" in order to feel prepared.

DURING THE EXAM

It can be unnerving to sit down and prepare to take a test or exam. Many students find the anxiety that accompanies them leading up to and when they begin an exam is so intense they forget the information they studied. There are strategies you can practice that will help you remain calm and focused during the exam period. Before you begin to explore new behaviors, consider the things you already do to ensure you have a successful test experience.

My 3 most effective strategies during a test are:

1. ....

....

....

....

2. ....

....

....

....

3. ....

....

....

....

The simplest advice professors can give students is to be there for the test. Administering an exam is a significant process for faculty. When students miss the exam period, it is challenging to find a fair method to allow one student to make up the test. At the start of the semester, make note of the test days on each of your syllabi. If you see any conflicts with an activity you have already scheduled, discuss it with your professor well in advance of the testing period. If you have an emergency come up on test day, do your best to contact your professor and explain your situation.

Be sure that you have all of the materials you will need for the test. If your test is open-book or open-notes, you should have your materials well organized so they can be referenced quickly and easily. If you are expected to complete the test in pencil, be sure you have what you need as well as a spare. If you are authorized to use a calculator, be sure the batteries are fresh and that it is functioning properly. Consult your syllabus to remind yourself of any instructor requests for test sessions, such as a blue book or a particular type of paper that should be used. These may seem like common-sense reminders; however, your mental preparation can be easily disrupted if you find yourself in a panic because you do not have the necessary materials.

- *If this is not your first test in the course, review your previous tests and the professor's feedback to remind yourself of the types of questions the professor asked, as well as any feedback he or she included with your grade.*
- *If you find yourself crunched for time, try to identify the material you think is most likely to be covered, and focus on that.*

Tips for Reducing Test Anxiety During an Exam

- ***Select a seat*** *where you will have minimal distractions.*
- ***Take deep, relaxing breaths*** *and allow yourself to replace your anxious thoughts with relaxing ones.*
- ***Take your time.*** *There is no reward for turning in your test first.*
- ***Listen carefully*** *to instructions and read over the test thoroughly. You do not want to give incorrect answers because you misunderstood the instructions.*
- ***Use positive thoughts*** *to reassure yourself that you are prepared and will do well on the test.*
- ***Don't panic!*** *If you need to step away from the exam to calm your nerves, ask the professor if you can step out to get a drink of water.*

Once the testing period begins, take a few minutes and read through the entire test before you begin working. As you review the test, make note of the directions on each section, identify the point values for each type of section, note any areas that you are most confident about as well as any concepts for which you may be less-prepared. Taking a few moments to review the entire test can help eliminate any surprises as you progress through the exam period, and can also help you determine which items you should answer first.

It is a good idea to start with the items you are most confident about and then move on to those you feel less sure of. Don't linger too long on any one question; if you are unsure of an answer, make a notation by that item and move on. You can return to these items as you proofread your test. If you have questions about an item or do not understand what is being asked, ask the professor for clarification. By starting with the questions you are sure of, you help keep your confidence high and may find that the answer to one of the items you were less sure of comes to you as you make your way through the test.

If your test has multiple sections, there may be different instructions for each section. Remember to thoroughly read and re-read the directions before you begin work in any area. In addition to carefully following directions, look for key words that can help you determine how to respond to the item. For example, if you are prompted to "describe" a concept, you should give a detailed account of the information. If you are asked to "outline" an idea, you would use a more informal form of identifying key concepts and supplemental ideas without using complete sentences. If you are asked to "diagram" a concept, you should present a graph or chart and include any necessary explanations of the image. There are many ways your instructor can ask you to present what you know, so be sure to answer the specific question that is being asked in the format the information is requested.

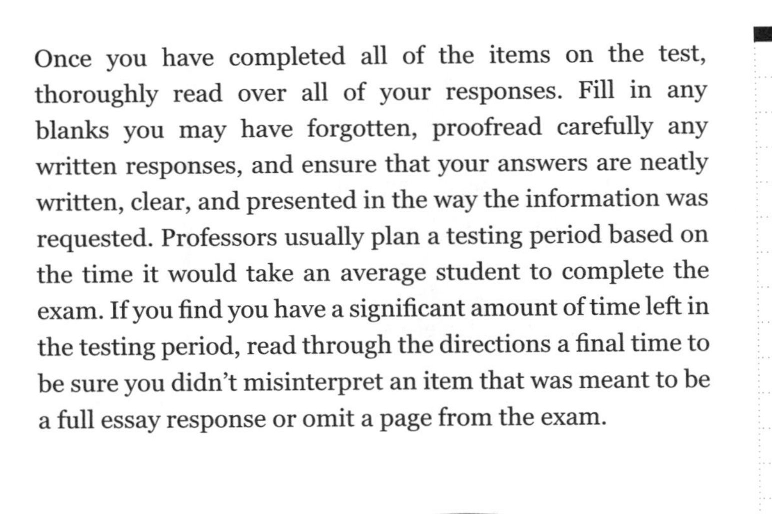

Once you have completed all of the items on the test, thoroughly read over all of your responses. Fill in any blanks you may have forgotten, proofread carefully any written responses, and ensure that your answers are neatly written, clear, and presented in the way the information was requested. Professors usually plan a testing period based on the time it would take an average student to complete the exam. If you find you have a significant amount of time left in the testing period, read through the directions a final time to be sure you didn't misinterpret an item that was meant to be a full essay response or omit a page from the exam.

Keeping it Together: Identifying and Managing Test Anxiety

A moderate level of apprehension leading up to and during an exam is expected in most students. The pressure of a testing situation can be daunting! Some students, however, experience more intense levels of nervousness and even fearfulness that can indicate a condition known as test anxiety. Students who experience test anxiety suffer emotional and physical reactions to testing situations and, if not identified and managed, can lead to lower performance on tests.

Consider these questions to determine if you suffer from test anxiety:

	YES OR NO	
1. *I feel like I can never study enough and find myself cramming for a test right up to the testing period.*	**Y**	**N**
2. *As I am studying for a test, I find myself thinking, "It's not worth it. I am never going to pass."*	**Y**	**N**
3. *I have trouble sleeping the night before a test.*	**Y**	**N**
4. *I feel physically ill (nausea, fast pulse, muscle tension) in the time leading up to a test.*	**Y**	**N**
5. *When I sit down to take a test, I break a sweat or have clammy hands.*	**Y**	**N**
6. *No matter how prepared I am, I often forget the information I studied when I am taking a test.*	**Y**	**N**
7. *I often feel overwhelmed by the pressure to perform well on a test.*	**Y**	**N**
8. *When I leave a test environment, I feel regret for many of my answers rather than feeling confident about my responses.*	**Y**	**N**

If you answered "yes" to any of these questions, you may suffer from test anxiety.

The first step to overcoming test anxiety is to recognize how and when it affects you. If you experience most of your anxiety during the time leading up to the exam, there are strategies that may help boost your confidence in your abilities as a test-taker. If you find that you start to get anxious as you prepare for your test, be sure that you include exercise in your weekly routine. Students who participate in a regular exercise program are less likely to experience anxiety in many areas of their lives, including academically stressful situations. As you prepare for the exam, focus on positive thoughts. Developing a positive attitude about the test situation can help reduce your feelings of anger toward the situation. Tests are a part of the college experience—you can't change that so you must learn how to cope with it. Get to class about five minutes early so you can relax for a few moments before the test is distributed. Do not arrive too early, however, as other students who are discussing the information or having a last-minute cram session may cause you to doubt yourself and your preparation. Stay confident and positive as you enter the testing situation!

If you have practiced positive thinking, are well prepared, and enter the testing environment with confidence but begin to experience anxiety once you begin taking your test, you may need to take a break from the test and focus on calming yourself. Close your eyes and take a few deep breaths to help clear your mind and refocus your attention on your exam. Identify a place that is calming and relaxing, such as the seashore or your favorite grassy spot on campus. Picture this place and try to remember the feelings of calmness and relaxation you have when you are there. Reassure yourself using positive thoughts such as, "I am prepared for this test. I know the information and am going to remain calm and make it through the test period."

The most effective way to fight test anxiety is with thorough preparation. Students who are well prepared for tests have higher confidence and experience less self-doubt, which is often to blame for feelings of anxiousness. If you suffer from test anxiety, it is even more important that you are intentional in your study time leading up to a test and that you study regularly between exam periods.

The tips presented here can help you combat test anxiety and the feeling of being overwhelmed by testing situations.

AFTER THE EXAM

One way to decrease your anxiety toward tests is to celebrate when you have successfully completed a testing situation. In order to prepare for your test, you adjusted your normal schedule, made sacrifices to be sure you had plenty of time to study, and remained focused on accomplishing your goal. Do not leave the test location and dwell on your performance. There is nothing you can do about the test, and until you receive your grade, you cannot have an accurate reaction to your performance. You may want to talk to other students and compare your reactions to the test. You will likely find that you were not alone in the items that you struggled with. If you do not take the time to reward yourself, you may find that your dread toward preparing for and taking tests only increases.

When you receive your graded test, review the questions you missed and identify any revisions you would make if given the opportunity. You may see some of your test items again on future exams, so it is worth your time to review what you wrote and be sure that you understand why you lost any points. If your professor will allow it, hang on to your graded test and all of your study materials so you can use them to prepare for the final exam.

Celebrating the end of a test period also helps keep you motivated to stick to your study schedule. You can remind yourself, "I have to stay in tonight to prepare for my test, but I will reward myself on Friday night with a trip to the movies with my friends." Set a goal now for how you will celebrate the next time you create a test preparation plan, follow the plan, and successfully complete a test.

Next time I complete a test I will celebrate by:

....

....

....

....

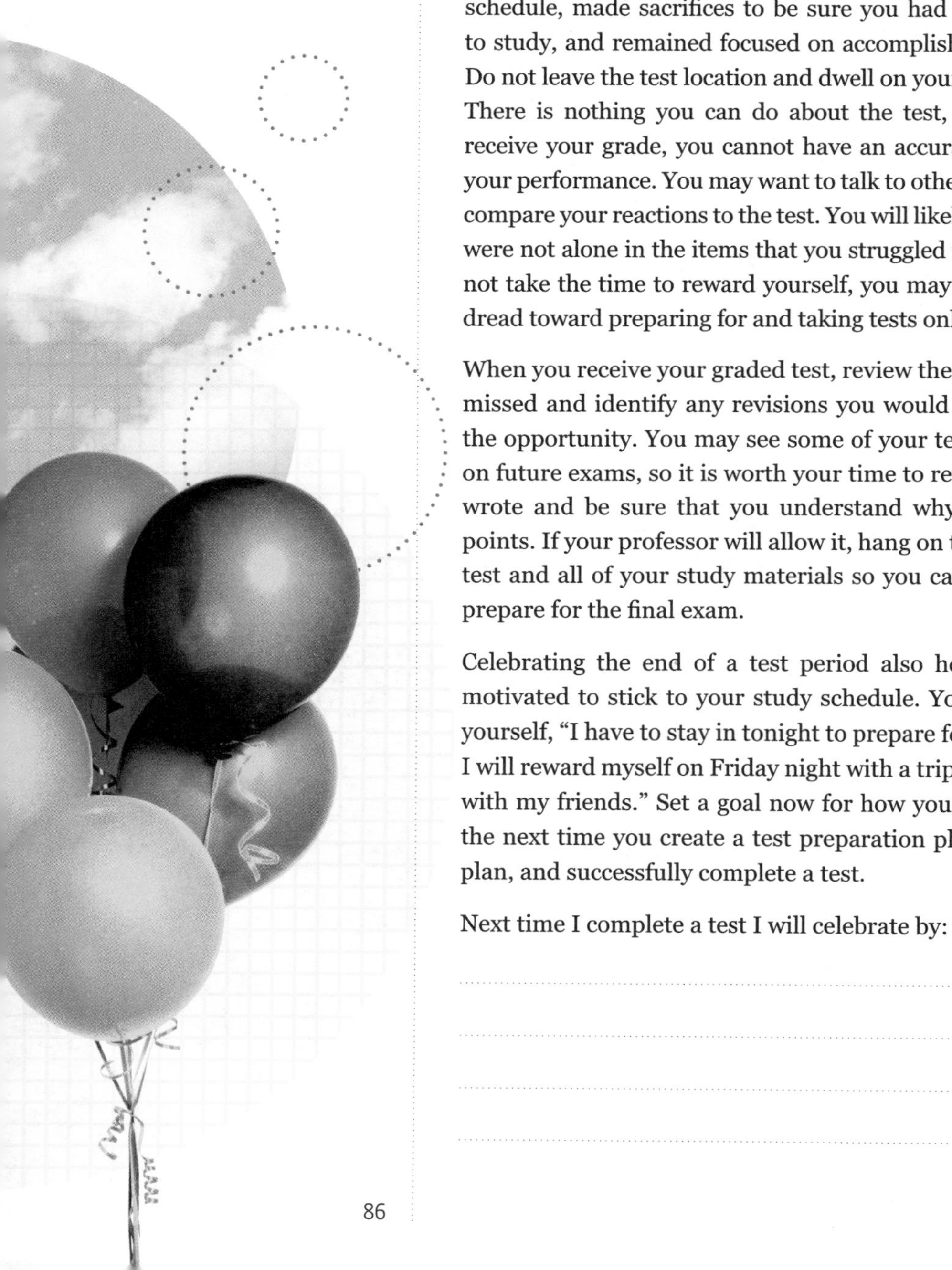

CHAPTER 9

Personal Planning & Goal-Setting

College. You've made it through high school, taken your standardized tests, and navigated the Common Application. So now what?

Most people haven't thought much about what they want out of college, and that's a huge mistake. Your college years are incredibly important, and there are a million ways you can spend your time: preparing for a career or further study, developing friendships and relationships, discovering new interests, hanging out with friends, playing sports, and many other activities.

With all these options, college goes by pretty fast. So you need to start thinking early—before you even arrive on campus, if you can—about what you want out of your years at college. It may seem like overkill now, but it's not hard, and you'll be glad you did.

As Early as Possible (Ideally Before You Get to Campus!)

The first step is to think big-picture. Ask yourself some basic questions:

- *How do I envision my time at college?*
- *What do I want to do while I'm there?*
- *What am I interested in, and what do I want to study?*
- *What activities, sports, etc., do I want to be involved in?*
- *What do I see myself doing after college?*

Write down what you're thinking. Congratulations, now you have goals! Then talk about them with people who know you well—parents, coaches, friends, employers, and teachers. Tell them what you're thinking, and ask them what they think. They'll help you figure out what's most important, and what you need to do once you get to campus (and after...). The most important thing is to get a basic idea of what you want to accomplish during your time in college. See, that wasn't so bad.

Early in your first semester

Now it's time to get a little more specific. You're on campus, and you're starting to settle in. Now you need to take your big-picture goals and start to translate them into action. But don't zero in just yet. Take the goals you've outlined, refined by conversations with people who know you well, and seek out advice from people on campus. Most colleges and universities have someone (like a Dean) responsible for first-year students—seek them out. Also look for career counselors, subject advisors (like for pre-med, pre-law, pre-business, etc.), and older students who offer to serve as mentors. Go talk to them—tell them your broad goals for college, and ask them what you should do to get there. Ask them if they have any other advice or suggestions for you. Finally, ask them who else you should talk to. Pretty soon, just by talking to these people, you'll start to develop some specific ideas about what you need to do to accomplish your goals. Plus, you're starting to get noticed on campus!

You should also start having a good idea of how you need to divide up your time. You'll definitely have class and homework, but what else? Practice? Extracurricular activities? Time with a best friend or significant other? Every college student has more things to do than they can possibly accomplish in a 24-hour (or a 4-year) period. The key to doing as much as possible is scheduling. You should start developing a daily and weekly schedule, and adjust it as needed. There are a few keys to making a good schedule:

- ***Prioritization:*** *Determine what you* have *to get done, and make sure those things get done first.*
- ***Personalization:*** *Figure out when in your day and week is the best time to do particular things. If you're a morning person, reading or studying before class may be more effective than late at night. If you're an athlete and likely to be too exhausted after practice to do homework, do it before practice.*
- ***Packaging:*** *A lot of things, like writing a term paper, seem like big jobs that you just really don't feel like doing right now. Unfortunately, that feeling often persists until the last minute. But there's an easier way! Package big jobs into small ones. Writing your term paper involves many steps, which in themselves don't take all that much time: thinking about a topic, researching it, writing an introduction, body, conclusion, proofreading, etc. Instead of doing all this in a 12-hour period (or even less), try spreading it out over a week. Spread your*

research over two days, write your intro the next day, your body the day after that, and then your conclusion. Repackaged like this, your term paper is a much more manageable, enjoyable job, and you can even be proud of the final product.

- ***Blocking:*** *Think in terms of blocks of time. If you have weekly problem sets that usually take three hours to complete, try to find a solid, three-hour chunk of time when you can sit down and do the whole thing. It's usually helpful to do specific things in a given block of time, and, if possible, at the same time of the day or week.*
- ***Diversifying:*** *The great thing about scheduling is it allows you to do a lot of things in a short period of time. Try to balance your schedule so that every day, and certainly every week, you include some time for homework, some for extracurriculars or practice, and time just for yourself and/or your friends.*
- ***Reward:*** *The point of making a schedule is so you can combine the things you* have *to do with as many of the things you* want *to do as possible. Try to schedule time with friends, a meal, or something fun after you finish a particular task.*

It will probably take a few weeks to work out a good schedule—that's fine. If you need help, many colleges and universities have a Learning Resource Center, or something similarly named, that can help you with time management.

Okay, so now you have an idea of how to manage your time. Now you also need to make some decisions. The most important of these is which classes to take (because you've asked yourself the big questions, you have some idea of what you want to study, and what you want to do after college). Go get yourself a course catalog. Read through it—not every word, but don't just skim it, either. Get an idea of the range of courses and programs your college or university offers. Look for special courses, programs, or opportunities (like classes with field trips, field studies, etc.). Pay special attention to any grade requirements or prerequisites. Consider honors programs or programs that require particular academic qualifications; this will be very important if you want to go to graduate school. Here are three other pieces of advice on courses:

- *Take at least one course, preferably in your freshman year, in a subject you've never studied before. You may have goals, like being a doctor, that require you to take some specific classes or programs. But that doesn't mean you can't explore—and your tuition money will be just a little bit wasted if you don't study something new.*
- *Whenever possible, take classes based on the professor, not the subject. You'll probably have required courses and prerequisites; fine. But when you have a choice, choose the professor with the best reputation for being a good teacher. A poor teacher can make the most fascinating topic as dull as dirt, whereas a great teacher can make anything interesting. Also, you'll want to be on the lookout for professors you respect and admire to write you letters of recommendation (hopefully the feeling is mutual!). Make sure you stay in touch with these professors.*
- *In general, the smaller the class or program, the better. You're more likely to get specialized attention, and it will probably be easier to get to know your classmates and professors (the latter is helpful for getting good letters of recommendation, which almost everyone will need at some point).*

Finally, make sure you're aware of people at your college or university who can help you. Almost every college or university has an advising system; use it! Also, if you have special needs or concerns, such as being an international student, a student with disabilities, or a nontraditional student, look for centers or offices that can help you. Most colleges and universities have centers or offices devoted to helping students with special

needs or concerns. If you're an athlete, most programs will have special academic and advising resources for you. Make sure to use them—it's often tough to balance sports and school, and they will be there to help.

In Your First Semester and Early in Your Second Semester

So, now you're really starting to get a feel for what college is like. Fortunately, you're ahead of almost everyone, because you've planned and learned to structure your time well. Unlike most people around you, you get your work done and have time to hang out. But there are still important decisions to be made, and several things to consider.

First, extracurriculars: Consider the following major types of activities, which often lead to opportunities during the summers and after graduation (if not the discovery of a new passion): student government, theater and performing arts, sports, campus journalism, international affairs and advocacy (Amnesty International, Global Affairs Club, etc.), academic competition (Quiz Bowl, Mock Trial, debate, etc.), community service, and honors societies. You won't have time for everything, but try out at least a few activities—you might never have the opportunity again.

Second, jobs: A lot of students need money for college. But the time you work takes away from time spent learning, hanging out with friends, and many of the best things about college. So, here are two thoughts on working during college:

- ***Avoid menial jobs if at all possible.*** *They're usually exhausting, they don't improve your résumé, and you usually don't earn much anyway. The alternative? Consider working as a research assistant for a professor, for the admissions office, or something that will add directly to your academic or professional skills.*
- ***Look for internships and special job experiences.*** *Some of them are paid; many are not. But they often do provide valuable experience and skills that will help you a lot more than working in a restaurant.*

Of course, these things are sometimes easier said than done. If you're pressed for money, go have a chat with your college or university financial aid office, and see what they can do for you. Also, do a Google search and see if your state has a Higher Education Fund, a Higher Education Financing Authority, or something similar that can help you out. Always, always avoid private loans—they often have very high interest rates. Also, be aware that the higher your grades are, the more likely someone will be willing to fund you!

Third, since the end of the school year is beginning to appear on the horizon, use the summers! Look for internship, research, and travel experiences. Your college or university should have several offices that will help (often called things like Undergraduate Research, Career Services, Honors, Special Programs, etc.). If in doubt, go to the Dean of the College of Arts and Sciences (or equivalent). There are a lot of special programs that are just for students in college. Take it from a recent college graduate: take advantage of these while you can! Whatever you do, don't spend the summers at home on the couch.

In Your Second, Third, and Fourth Years

So, you've completed several semesters of college. You've learned to manage your time well, and have been getting a lot out of your experience. But you should also think about what comes next. Because you started planning way early, you've been ahead of your peers in thinking about what you want to do after college, and you've structured your time, courses, activities, and programs accordingly. But you also need to make sure you pay attention to some specifics.

First, if you haven't already, sit down with someone from Career Services (or a similar organization at your school) and discuss how you can prepare yourself for moving in that direction. Tell them what your postcollege plans are, and discuss how you can prepare yourself for moving in that direction. Ask them to go over your résumé, and to help you practice your interview skills.

Second, renew relationships with professors, and ask for letters of recommendation. The earlier you do this, the better. Be specific about what you want the letter to say, and who the audience is. Think about what you want the professor to highlight, in terms of your skills, accomplishments or abilities, and request the professor to include these things.

Third, network! Your college or university will have an alumni network; this is your first stop. Look up people who have careers similar to what you want to do, and get in touch. Alums are usually happy to offer some advice. Also, ask your professors for contacts they have, and ask them to provide you with an introduction. Friends, coaches, internship supervisors, and the like can also be good networking resources.

Late in Your Fourth Year and on Graduation Day

Relax. You've planned and managed your time well, and you've gotten what you wanted out of college. You've gotten your work done and had time left over for extracurricular and fun. And because you've done all that, you'll be able to go on and do whatever it is you want to do after college. **This is your reward for setting goals, and planning and managing your time.**

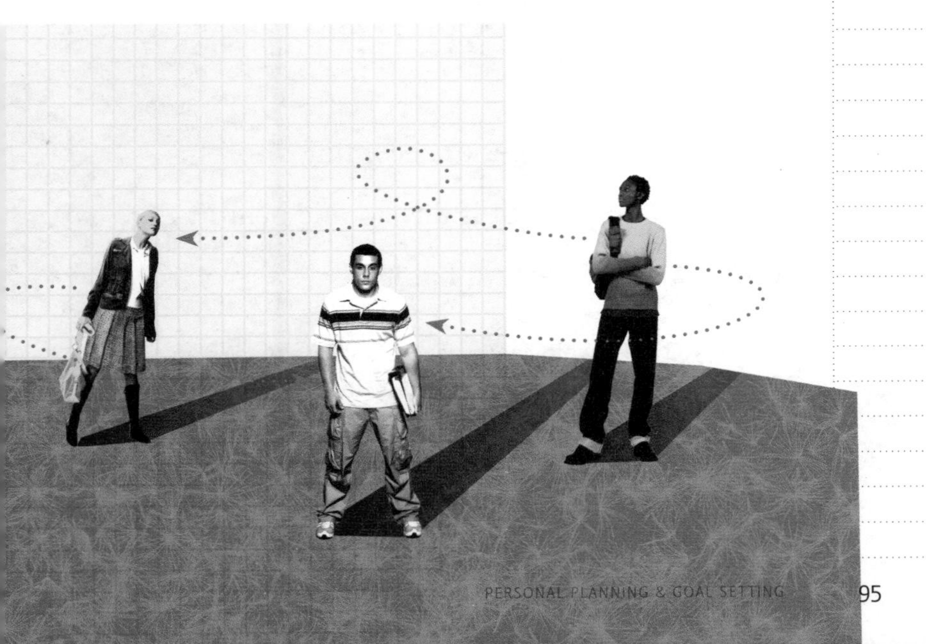

CHAPTER 10

Financial Responsibility

One of the challenges of becoming an independent student is developing healthy financial-management habits.

Just as you are learning how to successfully manage your time and your academic and social responsibilities, you must also learn to effectively manage your financial responsibilities.

Creating and Following a Personal Budget

The key to responsible money management is successful budgeting. Keeping an accurate record of your income and your spending will ensure that you are prepared for unexpected expenses that may occur during the semester, and also help you plan for occasions when you want to spend a little extra on something for yourself like a new university hoodie or tickets to see your favorite band.

The first step to setting up a personal budget is to identify all of your *income resources*. This may include money you receive from scholarships or grants, earnings from your on- or off-campus job, money you receive from your family, and savings you have collected prior to beginning college. Once you have a clear record of your income sources, you can plan for your expenses or expenditures. Your *fixed expenses* are bills that you pay on a regular basis such as tuition, fees for room and board or rent, car insurance, and semester parking fees. You can anticipate that these bills will come regularly and that you will know ahead of time the dates they will be due. Fixed expenses should take top priority in your budget plan. Once you determine that you have the funds for the fixed expenses, you can plan for your *variable expenses*. These are usually more discretionary purchases such as entertainment (e.g. dining out; movies, plays and concerts; school supplies; clothing) and, while they are important, you are less likely to anticipate their exact amount.

If you have never created a budget, it is a good idea to practice tracking your spending for a short period of time. Write down everything that you spend for a week, then two weeks, then a month. Creating a short-term spending plan can help you create an accurate budget for a full semester or academic year.

Obtaining Your Credit History

It is a good idea to occasionally check your credit history and you can do this at no charge through a government-supported Web site. Once a year you can visit annualcreditreport.com or call 1-877-322-8228 to obtain a free copy of your credit history. Beware of companies that may advertise free credit reports as they often carry a membership fee.

Budget Breakdown

INCOME RESOURCES (For academic year)

Financial assistance (loans, scholarships, grants) .... ________

Support/allowances from family .... ________

Savings from pre-college earnings .... ________

Part-time job earnings .... ________

Other .... ________

Total income resources: .... ________

ESTIMATED FIXED EXPENSES (For academic year)

Tuition and fees x 2 semesters .... ________

Textbooks and supplies x 2 semesters .... ________

On-campus room x 2 semesters .... ________

On-campus meal plan x 2 semesters .... ________

Car payment and insurance x 9 months .... ________

Parking fees x 2 semesters .... ________

Other (x 2 semesters or x 9 if monthly) .... ________

Total fixed expenses: .... ________

ESTIMATED VARIABLE EXPENSES (For academic year)

Travel expenses (gasoline, flight, train tickets) x 9 months .... ______

Clothing and accessories x 9 months .... ______

Health and beauty expenses
(medication, cosmetics, grooming supplies, haircuts) x 9 months .... ______

Cellular phone fees x 9 months .... ______

Entertainment
(tickets to sporting events, music downloads, dining out, movies) x 9 months .... ______

Other x 9 months .... ______

Total variable expenses: .... ______

BUDGET RESULTS

Total estimated resources .... ______

Total estimated fixed expenses plus .... ______

Total estimated variable expenses .... + ______

Total estimated expenses .... = ______ → − ______

Balance (or deficit): .... = ______

Becoming a Savvy Spender:

TIPS FOR SAVING

Eliminate or reduce fees for services you are not using. *If you find that you are not using all of the meals on your meal plan, contact dining services to see if you can reduce your plan or shift some of your meal money to a more flexible account. You may also find that you have more cell phone minutes in your plan than you actually need. Reducing your cellular plan can help you balance the discretionary side of your budget.*

Use your meal plan. *If you live on campus, you likely have a prepaid meal plan that allows you to eat at the campus dining facilities a number of times a week. It can be tempting to go out to dinner with friends but when you skip meals on campus, you are throwing away money that you have already paid through your meal plan. Consider eating on campus and then joining friends after dinner for a movie. You will save money on dinner, allowing you to get the large popcorn at the show!*

Identify places where you can save money. *Sleep in and save a few bucks when you brew your own java. If you stop in the campus coffee shop each morning and purchase a cup of joe for $2.50, you will spend nearly $200 over the course of the semester! If you purchase a coffee pot for $20 and a couple pounds of fresh ground coffee for under $10, you can make your own coffee each morning saving $170 over a 15-week semester and hours of time standing in line.*

(CONT'D)

Building Good Credit: You can Start Now!

Once you have a grasp on your personal budget and you are able to anticipate your monthly spending and cover your expenses with your income, you may consider opening a credit account in your name. Credit card usage is one of the ways you can begin to build your credit rating. Your credit score is like your character. It is an indicator to potential lenders and potential employers that you are a responsible spender and borrower. A good credit rating can open many doors for you, including helping you land a job, and acceptance for a car or home loan at a low interest rate. However, just as a good credit rating can open many doors, a poor credit rating can hinder your ability to make major financial transactions.

Your credit rating is referred to as your FICO score (named for the Fair Isaac Corporation, credited with creating the first system for rating credit history). Your FICO score can range from 300 to 850. Scores of 700 or higher are considered excellent in most lending situations. Most lenders look for scores in the high 600s or better. There are many things that can affect your credit rating and it is your responsibility to establish and maintain a high score. You have control over most of the components that determine your credit score. Making payments on time, such as your credit card and car payments, will help increase your credit score. Paying off any debts, such as the balance on a credit card, will also contribute to a positive score. Just as these actions can help your credit rating, failure to make payments on time or carrying a high balance on a card can have an adverse affect on your credit score.

It is never too early to begin thinking about your credit score and establishing a trustworthy credit history. Many employers will ask for a credit report as part of the hiring process as a high credit score indicates that you are a responsible spender and that you accept accountability for your debts. While it may seem a long way off, in just a few short years you may wish to purchase a home or make another large purchase like a vehicle or furniture for your house or apartment. A few mistakes on your credit history like a missed credit card payment or late submission of your monthly cellular phone bill could limit your ability to be approved for these types of transactions.

Credit Card Usage

Credit cards are a tool for establishing credit and may allow for more flexible spending for the items in your budget. Some of your expenses may be difficult to cover using cash or checks; credit cards can help you make purchases online, like discounted textbooks or concert tickets. It is important that you use your credit cards wisely so that you stay within your budget and establish a credit score you can be proud of. Think of a credit card as a loan. You are borrowing money from the company that carries your card, with the promise to pay the money back. If you pay back the amount you borrow on a monthly basis, you avoid an interest fee. However, if you do not pay the full balance each month, or you get behind on your payments, you will pay an interest charge on the amount you borrowed, and that can add up quickly! Before you decide to open a credit account, consider how it will serve you as a budgeting tool. A credit card can be used to help you make purchases that you have budgeted for; however, it should not be used to supplement purchases that you do not have the income to support.

If your favorite band is coming to town you may consider using your credit card for the $100 ticket. As the concert date approaches, a quick trip to the mall could add $60 for a new pair of jeans (you have to look good, right?) to your balance. A final “must have” of $40 for a concert T-shirt and your concert experience has added $200 to your credit card balance. If you make only the minimum payment on your

Use your talents to help bring in more income. *You may or may not have the time for a part-time job, but you can identify ways to bring in extra money to help subsidize your spending habits. If you take organized and thorough notes, you may be able to serve as a note-taker for a student with a learning disability. Community members and professors often look to students to help with personal services like childcare, pet sitting, or house keeping. If you enjoy working out, consider spending a couple hours a week as a group fitness instructor. Check with the career services department and pay attention to fliers posted on campus for opportunities like these.*

Shop smarter for your textbooks. *There is a competitive market for textbooks and it is up to you to find the most cost-efficient method of purchasing your books each semester. Once you have registered for a course, check with the campus bookstore to see the required texts and resources and make note of the cost of each book. Then, determine which books may be available through other avenues such as online book distributors, the local bookstore, and competing bookstores near campus, and price them at several places. You may find that purchasing your books from an alternative source will save you money. However, before you select an off-campus book seller, pay attention to any shipping fees that may accompany your purchases and whether your financial aid is restricted to campus locations.*

card with an 18% interest rate (many cards carry a higher rate), it will take you 2 years to pay off your concert weekend. By then, the band will likely have broken up, making your T-shirt your new favorite dust rag.

If you already had a $300 balance on your card because you decided to charge your textbooks for the semester, your concert weekend will bring you to a $500 balance. That may not seem like much; however, if you make only the minimum payment on this balance, and make no new purchases, your time to pay off the card increases to 94 months—almost 8 years! Over the course of the 94 months, you will have paid $440 in interest.

The best way to manage a credit card is to use it only on items that you can cover 100% with your monthly income. If you find yourself with a growing credit card balance, stop spending and try to make more than the minimum payment each month. Your $500 balance on an 18% interest rate card will require about a $10 minimum monthly payment. If you are able to pay $30 a month, you can pay off your balance in just 20 months. This is more appealing than the 94 months it would take making only the minimum payment. You also save $340 in interest, paying only $100 in interest fees. Remember to include your credit card payment in the expenses area of your budget because you will not have this $30 to spend on your other monthly needs.

Financial Aid

Whether you have the assistance of your family or you are financing your education on your own, it is your responsibility to be knowledgeable about your financial aid options and to pursue support from other sources to help pay for your college expenses. Financial aid comes in many forms, including money that does not have to be repaid such as grants and scholarships, and money that is borrowed with the promise to repay the funds when you graduate. The staff in your financial aid office can help you determine what types of assistance you may qualify for. Visit your institution's financial aid Web site or make an appointment to meet with a counselor to explore your options and eligibility.

Grants are often funded by state or federal governments and do not require a repayment. Federal grant programs are often awarded based on students' needs and ability to pay for college. Like most forms of aid, federal grants carry a minimum GPA requirement to maintain your aid. Your eligibility for grants is most often determined through an analysis of your Free Application for Federal Student Aid (FAFSA) that must be completed annually. You will be expected to complete a FAFSA each year after you have filed your taxes to determine your eligibility for the next year. You can complete a new application or renew your annual FASFA by visiting the Federal Student Aid Web site at www.fafsa.ed.gov.

Scholarship funds are distributed through a diverse array of agencies and organizations. Your institution may have offered you a scholarship based on your academic achievements in high school or a talent that you bring to the campus community such as outstanding academic achievement, athletics, community service, or talent in the arts. While some scholarships are awarded at the start of your college career, there are many scholarships that you can apply for beyond your first year. Many scholarship programs are geared toward a particular population of students. You may find scholarship opportunities based on your major, career aspirations, your parents' employment, your gender, your region or hometown, or leadership experiences. With so many scholarship programs, it can be difficult to know where to start looking. A member of the financial aid staff at your institution can help you identify scholarship resources, but remember that many applications are due several months to a year in advance of the awarded term, so plan ahead and start looking for scholarships early.

Unlike grants and scholarships, student loans must be repaid when you either graduate or are no longer enrolled in college-level courses. If you accept a loan, you will be expected to pay back the principal amount of the loan as well as any accrued interest. You may qualify for a loan on your own or your parent or guardian may apply for a loan on your behalf. When you accept a student loan, you are borrowing against your future in that you are placing confidence in the fact that earning a college degree will help you secure a higher-paying position in your career field. The federal government regulates most student loans and the interest rates are often less than loans that are offered by private organizations or banks.

Nearly 80 percent of first-year college students receive some form of financial aid. If you need support financing your college education, there may be a source that can assist you. Your financial aid staff can help you identify the financial aid sources that are right for you and your unique financial needs.

Student Employment

Another way that you may choose to help fund your education is through on-campus employment. Having a job with a campus office or department can provide networking opportunities with administrators and faculty while learning and practicing the skills that are expected of professionals, such as strong written and oral communication skills, organizational skills, and the ability to manage multiple tasks at one time. Having a part-time job can also enhance your time-management skills as you will have to balance your work schedule with your other priorities.

Working part-time can have a positive effect on your overall college experience. Research supports that students who work on campus 20 hours a week or less have higher grades and report greater campus engagement than those who work more than 20 hours. Working too many hours may negatively affect your studies. Students who work more than 20 hours report that their job responsibilities interfere with their studies and, therefore, negatively affect their grades. Off-campus employers are not as likely to cooperate with the challenges of working around your class and activity schedule. Additionally, students who work off-campus do not see the same positive outcomes associated with working within the college environment, such as developing relationships with campus faculty and staff and learning about campus resources and the college environment.

When you explore the opportunity of campus employment, in addition to helping you finance your education, the skills that you develop and the relationships that you build may help you secure future employment. You may find information about campus employment opportunities in your campus career center, through your institution's human resources Web site, in the financial aid office, or within your academic department.

Conclusion

Most college students find themselves adjusting to a more frugal lifestyle than they were accustomed to at home. Living frugally for a few years will pay off when you graduate and begin your career with limited debt and the skills to manage a full-time salary with multiple expenses. Money-management habits such as effective budgeting and responsible credit card use can help you build a good credit history and prepare for a secure financial future.

References

National Center for Educational Statistics:
http://nces.ed.gov/FastFacts/display.asp?id=31

Inside Higher Ed June 8, 2009

CHAPTER 11

Wellness

What does wellness mean to you?

Perhaps it means you are physically fit or that you eat a balanced diet. Perhaps it means that you are free from illness or disease. Or, maybe it means you are living a life of minimal stress. Wellness is all of these things, and much more.

Being "well" is more than just eating right and exercising; truly being well means having a good quality of life that includes pursuing moderation, variety, and balance.

Consider wellness as a wheel that is divided into different dimensions that determine who you are and how you enjoy your life. The "spokes" of the wellness wheel include several components that help make you the person you are. Your overall wellness is comprised of your attitude and behavior with regard to your health in the following areas: physical, social, emotional, intellectual, occupational, and spiritual.

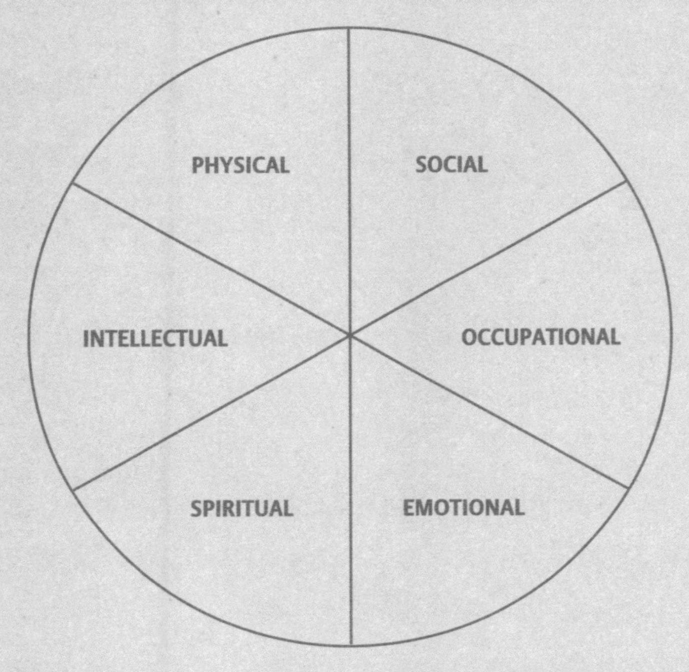

As you begin, consider these six areas of wellness as you respond to these items:

- *In which dimensions of life are you most well?*
- *In which dimensions are you least well?*

Just as effective time management requires planning, so does effective management of your health. When you consider the way you spend your time each day, do you see an adequate amount of time dedicated to keeping your body well?

You can likely identify areas of your overall wellness where you practice good behaviors as well as areas where you could use some improvement. Take a moment and reflect on your behaviors and make note of the things you already do to take care of yourself.

Wellness Assessment

List three things you do to keep yourself well in each of the following areas:

PHYSICAL

1. ....

2. ....

3. ....

SOCIAL

1. ....

2. ....

3. ....

EMOTIONAL

1. ....

2. ....

3. ....

INTELLECTUAL

1. ....

2. ....

3. ....

SPIRITUAL

1. ....

2. ....

3. ....

OCCUPATIONAL

1. ....

2. ....

3. ....

Physical Wellness

NUTRITION & EXERCISE

Your physical wellness is determined by the decisions you make with regard to your eating, sleeping, and exercise habits. Your physical health is also affected by your decisions with regard to alcohol and drug use, as well as sexual behaviors.

When you consider your level of physical health you probably think about nutrition most often. You can likely identify foods that are healthy versus those that contain little to no nutritional benefits, and you recognize that regular activity is an important part of living a healthy life. However, recognizing *how* to make healthy choices and actually *making* healthy choices are two different processes.

Do you know if your eating habits are healthy? Do you know what foods and nutrients are missing from your diet? A good place to start is to review the food pyramid developed by the U.S. Department of Agriculture at www.mypyramid.gov. Following the healthy eating guidelines will not only help you limit your weight gain but also help boost your fitness level and help you fight off illness. When you are a student, it can be challenging to plan your meals. Most of what you eat is prepared for you and you are limited by the offerings of the dining facilities on campus. Making healthy choices when you have access to so many unhealthy options can be challenging! One way to help limit your intake of unhealthy foods is to keep a food diary. For one week, write down everything you eat, portion sizes, and what category of the food pyramid it fits into. After the week of recording, review your diary and note the categories where you have not taken in the recommended servings.

Eat MORE of These!

- *Fruits and vegetables*
- *Baked potatoes or sweet potatoes with low-fat salad dressing, chili, or broccoli*
- *Honey whole-wheat roll or bread with turkey, veggies, and light mayo*
- *Lean roast beef sub with veggies on whole wheat, no mayo or oil*
- *Vegetarian entrees*
- *Salad bar salads with dark green leafy lettuce, lots of veggies, and low-fat salad dressing on the side*
- *Pasta dishes with tomato sauces*
- *Egg white omelets with veggies, topped with salsa*
- *Grilled or baked entrées like chicken and fish with a side of brown rice and veggies*
- *Veggie or soy burgers*
- *Vegetable stir-fry with or without chicken or shrimp*
- *Nonfat frozen yogurt for dessert*
- *Snacks like ginger snaps, graham crackers, pretzels, and unbuttered popcorn*

Eat LESS of These!

- *Pizza with extra meat*
- *Doughnuts and croissants*
- *Burgers and fries*
- *Cold-cut subs*
- *Eggs and bacon*
- *Hot dogs*
- *Macaroni and cheese*
- *Fried foods: chicken, fish, french fries, etc.*
- *Veggies covered with cream sauces and cream-based soups*

Daily Food Log (7-day assessment - Day 1)

DAY/DATE

Meal	Grains	Vegetables	Dairy	Fruits	Proteins
BREAKFAST					
LUNCH					
DINNER					
SNACK 1					
SNACK 2					
TOTAL DAILY SERVINGS					

NOTES

Daily Food Log (7-day assessment - Day 2)

DAY/DATE					
Meal	**Grains**	**Vegetables**	**Dairy**	**Fruits**	**Proteins**
BREAKFAST					
LUNCH					
DINNER					
SNACK 1					
SNACK 2					
TOTAL DAILY SERVINGS					
NOTES					

Daily Food Log (7-day assessment - Day 3)

DAY/DATE					
Meal	**Grains**	**Vegetables**	**Dairy**	**Fruits**	**Proteins**
BREAKFAST					
LUNCH					
DINNER					
SNACK 1					
SNACK 2					
TOTAL DAILY SERVINGS					
NOTES					

Daily Food Log (7-day assessment - Day 4)

DAY/DATE

Meal	Grains	Vegetables	Dairy	Fruits	Proteins
BREAKFAST					
LUNCH					
DINNER					
SNACK 1					
SNACK 2					
TOTAL DAILY SERVINGS					

NOTES

Daily Food Log (7-day assessment - Day 5)

DAY/DATE

Meal	Grains	Vegetables	Dairy	Fruits	Proteins
BREAKFAST					
LUNCH					
DINNER					
SNACK 1					
SNACK 2					
TOTAL DAILY SERVINGS					

NOTES

Daily Food Log (7-day assessment - Day 6)

DAY/DATE					
Meal	**Grains**	**Vegetables**	**Dairy**	**Fruits**	**Proteins**
BREAKFAST					
LUNCH					
DINNER					
SNACK 1					
SNACK 2					
TOTAL DAILY SERVINGS					
NOTES					

Daily Food Log (7-day assessment - Day 7)

DAY/DATE

Meal	Grains	Vegetables	Dairy	Fruits	Proteins
BREAKFAST					
LUNCH					
DINNER					
SNACK 1					
SNACK 2					
TOTAL DAILY SERVINGS					

NOTES

Reviewing a food diary can help you identify areas where you can improve your eating habits. For example, you may find that you like to enjoy a snack in the mid-afternoon. If you know you will want a snack around the same time each day, you can plan accordingly and pack a healthy snack such as a piece of fruit. Reaching into your backpack for your planned snack will save you both calories and money from the vending machine. (Your daily $.85 candy bar habit can add up to nearly $150 over the course of a school year!) It is important to remember that you do not need to eliminate any foods from your diet; even that piece of pizza can be an occasional indulgence. However, you should limit your intake of foods that are high in calories and fat and ensure that you are taking in an adequate amount of nutrition each day.

It is important that you pay attention to and plan appropriately for eating and exercising. However, over-thinking or obsessing about your eating can lead to very unhealthy behaviors. If you find yourself thinking about food all the time or exercising to excess, you may be at risk for an eating disorder and should seek professional assistance immediately.

Eating well is only the first step to achieving good physical wellness. The second step is to participate in a healthy level of activity. You can increase your activity level by making small adjustments to your daily habits. If you usually take the bus or shuttle to class, consider leaving a few minutes earlier to bike or walk across campus. You can save time and burn a few calories when you skip the elevator line and take the stairs to your residence hall room or class. Exercise doesn't have to be dreadful—it can and should be fun! You are more likely to participate in activities that you enjoy, so identify things that you find enjoyment from and include them in your weekly plan. For example, intramural sports are a great way to meet friends and can also be a fun way to increase your activity level. Including physical activity in your weekly plan may actually help you become a more successful student. People who include activity in their daily schedule see many benefits, including reduced stress, weight loss, higher quality sleep, and higher self-esteem.

RESPONSIBLE DECISIONS TOWARD ALCOHOL

College life offers new freedoms for many students. With your new freedom comes choices, including the decision of whether to consume alcohol. The culture of drinking on college campuses affects everyone in the community, even if you choose not to drink. When students choose to drink alcohol in an irresponsible manner, they may create problems that not only negatively affect the user, but also their friends, family, classmates, co-workers, and community members. It is everyone's responsibility to be actively involved in promoting a safe campus environment.

Alcohol is one of the most widely used drugs on college campuses. Data collected by the National Institute for Alcohol Abuse and Alcoholism (Hingson, et al, 2005) indicates:

- *1,700 college students between 18 and 24 die each year from alcohol-related injuries.*
- *599,000 students between 18 and 24 are injured while under the influence of alcohol each year.*
- *2.1 million students between 18 and 24 drive under the influence of alcohol each year.*
- *25% of college students experience negative academic consequences of their drinking including missing class, falling behind on course assignments, doing poorly on exams or papers, and receiving lower grades overall.*

Drinking Your Dollars

According to factsontap.org, the average college student spends $900 on alcohol in one year, which is half the amount spent on books!

In the chart below, fill in the number of drinks, the price per drink, and the total you spend on alcohol for each day of the week and total the amount for the entire week.

	# of drinks	Price per drink	Total
Sunday			
Monday			
Tuesday			
Wednesday			
Thursday			
Friday			
Saturday			
Month total: Total for week x 4			
Year total: Month total x 12			
College total: Year total x 4			

Think of all the things you could purchase for the same amount of money that you spend on alcohol!

Tips When Getting Tipsy

You don't need to have alcohol to have fun! *If you do choose to drink, consider these tips to ensure you are acting responsibly and keeping yourself and your peers safe:*

- *If consuming alcohol, know what you are drinking. Bring your own beverages to a party and keep any open containers in your possession at all times. It is never a good idea to drink from a community cooler!*
- *Count your drinks and know your limits. You can keep up with how many drinks you have had by keeping the caps or tabs of your drinks in your pocket, and stopping when you have reached your limit.*
- *Slow down, don't chug. Instead, space your drinks and alternate alcoholic drinks with non-alcoholic beverages.*
- *Make sure you eat! It will help with the absorption of alcohol and may prevent you from experiencing alcohol poisoning.*
- *Designated drivers should not be drinking for 24 hours. If your DD decides to have a drink, even one, find an alternative ride home. Sober drivers should be completely sober for a full day before they take responsibility for safely getting you home!*

(CONT'D)

Binge Drinking

Students who choose to use alcohol responsibly drink within the limits of the law, in a safe environment, and consume only a reasonable amount of alcohol in one setting. However, some students choose to consume alcohol in large quantities over a short period of time. This is known as binge drinking. According to the Core Alcohol and Other Drug National Survey (2006), 47% of all college students reported engaging in binge drinking in the previous two weeks. Health professionals consider drinking five or more servings of alcohol during one episode to be classified as binge drinking. Consuming high-risk amounts of alcohol can lead to unwanted health problems, including blackouts, nausea and vomiting, and other serious consequences related to alcohol poisoning. These problems affect not only the individual, but also can have a profound ripple effect on the entire campus community.

There are many students who, after considering the risks associated with alcohol use, choose to minimize their drinking or abstain from drinking completely. These students are not free from the effects of alcohol. The profound effects of binge drinking cause many non-binging students to pay the price for this high-risk behavior. The following experiences are examples of the serious effects of second-hand binge drinking:

- *Having one's studying or sleep interrupted.*
- *Having to babysit or care for a drunken friend or roommate.*
- *Being insulted or humiliated by a drunk peer.*
- *Being confronted with unwanted sexual advances.*
- *Being in a serious argument or quarrel with a drunken peer.*
- *Being pushed, hit, or assaulted.*
- *Having one's property damaged.*
- *Being a victim of sexual assault or date rape.*

As with other decisions you will make with regard to your personal wellness, whether you will use alcohol, how often, and to what degree, is a choice you will have to make. It is important you make this decision only after you have considered the impact it will have on your overall wellness, including your academic success, your physical health, and your relationships with others.

Emotional Wellness

Another component of your overall wellness is the extent to which you are aware of and accept your feelings. Your emotional wellness is often indicated by your mood. When you are emotionally well, you feel positive and enthusiastic about life. You have a positive self-image, recognize the value of your life, and manage your stress well.

Think of the times in your life when you feel your best. Perhaps it is during holidays or celebrations when you are surrounded by people who care about you, or when you spend time working on a project for a club or organization you are passionate about and are recognized with a sign of gratitude from a peer. It feels good to do well and, when you are proud of yourself and the work you have done, your level of emotional wellness increases. Recognizing the activities and experiences that make you feel good about yourself and making time for those activities can help you stay emotionally well.

- *Don't mix alcohol with other drugs. The interactions of many drugs with alcohol can be very dangerous and even deadly.*
- *Be aware of unexpected costs of drinking! Before you head out, set a limit for how much you are going to spend. Take only that amount with you so you can monitor the expenses associated with drinking.*
- *Know the consequences of your choices. There are many legal repercussions associated with underage drinking. If you are not the legal age and you choose to drink, you should first consider the laws and consequences associated with underage drinking. Underage drinking is punishable by law and often carries with it hefty fines and, in some states, can be punishable by jail time.*

Benefits of Community Service:

- *Gain the satisfaction of helping others*
- *Develop skills that will transfer to your future career*
- *Gain exposure to cultural and socio-economic differences*
- *Learn civic and social responsibility for your community and the world*
- *Develop a deeper sense of yourself, including your skills and passions*
- *Develop meaningful connections with peers and community organizations*

Whether you enjoy running up and down a sports field, reading to children, expressing yourself through art or music, or helping keep the environment clean, you owe it to yourself to include in your daily plan the activities that bring you joy.

When you feel stress coming on and need a "pick me up," review your schedule and you will likely find that you have allocated very little time for the activities that give you gratification or bring you happiness. While it may seem that taking time away from your "to do" list will only add to your stress, you are more likely to find that balancing your time with activities you must do but do not get enjoyment, from with activities that bring you enjoyment will not only ensure that you feel well, but will make you a more balanced and effective learner.

STRESS

Just as you can identify the way you feel when you are emotionally well, you should also be able to identify emotions or feelings that indicate an imbalance in your emotional health. A decrease in your emotional health is most often caused by an increase in your level of stress. A major factor in your emotional wellness is your stress level. Stress is the result of the activities that go along with our daily life. Feelings of stress can be positive or negative, and you can often control these feelings with the way you respond to stressful situations. Some stress can be helpful; it keeps you motivated and helps you continue to work toward your goals. However, stress to the point of "distress" can impact your life to the point that it becomes difficult to achieve any of your goals.

Indicators of emotional distress are different for everyone. When you are feeling down, you may feel physically tired or fatigued, while others may feel high-strung or anxious. It is important that you recognize signs of negative stress in yourself so you can address the issue before it becomes distressful. Distress can get out of hand and cause health problems ranging from headaches and fatigue to depression and suicidal thoughts or tendencies.

How do you know when you are stressed?

List the characteristics you notice about yourself when you are feeling stressed and the coping strategies you use to combat your stress:

Situations that cause me stress:

My body responds to stress by:

I am able to manage my stress by:

ACHIEVING WELLNESS THROUGH COMMUNITY SERVICE

One method of enhancing your emotional wellness is through service to others. Today's college students recognize the value of service toward others and their community. According to The American Freshman report (HERI, 2007), incoming students rated the "importance of helping others" the highest it has been in twenty years. During your college experience you will have many opportunities to engage in community service and to reap the benefits of altruism.

Many of the outcomes of community service contribute to an enhanced level of emotional wellness. Participating in community service allows you to act within challenging environments while applying skills and knowledge that you gain in the classroom. It also allows you the opportunity to develop your character and a sense of civic responsibility. Service activities are a great way to explore your new surroundings. Students who participate in community service are more likely to feel connected to their community. Additionally, you may find yourself energized by the opportunity to use your talents to help others in need.

Social Wellness

College life is not all about academic success, it is also one of the most exciting times in your life! You have heard the phrase, "All work and no play makes Jack a dull boy." Your need for social interaction and the degree to which you feel you are part of your community contribute to your social wellness. You have the unique opportunity to explore your independence while surrounded by peers who are experiencing similar transitions. Making friends and developing healthy relationships is a major component of the college experience and can help you become a more well-rounded and healthy student.

One of the keys to making the most out of college is to identify activities that will enhance your experience while contributing to your future goals. Your institution hosts a variety of clubs and organizations that allow you to showcase your talents or to develop new skills. It is a good idea to identify a few events or activities that interest you and fit into your schedule. If you have a particular interest, consult your student organizations list and determine if there is a club dedicated to your interest. College is also about exploring new talents, so if you have a slight interest in a new hobby, find a related organization and attend one of the meetings to learn more. Try out numerous clubs and organizations before settling and becoming dedicated to just a few. Make the most of your time outside of the classroom by committing your time and energy to clubs and organizations that are the most beneficial and enriching to you, both professionally and personally.

Joining a student organization is just one example of how you can meet new and interesting people while enhancing your social wellness. Most activities that enhance your physical and emotional wellness can also impact your social wellness. Participation on a sports team, for example, will not only benefit your physical wellness but also allow you the opportunity to meet other students and make friends. Likewise, spending your spring break participating in a relief project in an area that has been affected by disaster impacts your emotional wellness while also allowing you to interact with other students and community members. With all there is to do and so many new opportunities to explore, it can be easy to get caught up in the social benefits of college life. Too much focus on your social wellness will throw your wellness wheel off balance! As you find a few activities you enjoy, incorporate them into your routine to help balance your overall wellness. But be cautious not to get so caught up in the social aspects of college life that you neglect the other aspects of overall wellness.

Intellectual And Occupational Wellness

Two areas of wellness that are closely related are intellectual and occupational wellness. Your intellectual wellness comes from the degree to which you engage your mind in creative and stimulating activities. Your occupational wellness is determined by the satisfaction you receive from your work or, as a student, your course of study.

You likely had some expectations about your academic experiences as you began your college career. For example, based on your experiences in high school and knowing your areas of strength, you may have expected that some of your courses would be more challenging than others. Additionally, you may have been looking forward to exploring your career choice or, if you have not decided on a career, exploring the breadth of opportunities that are available for you.

- *Think about your expectations for your academic work.*
- *What classes did you expect to most enjoy in college?*
- *What classes did you expect would give you the greatest challenge?*
- *What did you expect your professors to be like?*
- *Now consider how your academic experience, thus far, has compared to what you expected.*
- *How satisfied are you with the level of academic challenge you are receiving? Is it too much? Too little?*
- *Do you find your coursework to be meaningful?*
- *Do you see the relevance between what you are learning and how you will apply that learning to your life?*

EXPLORING YOUR MAJOR

Consider your responses to the questions on the previous page. If you have found that your expectations for your academic experience have been met, you find your work challenging yet meaningful, and you are satisfied with your courses, you likely feel "well" with regard to your intellectual experiences. If, however, you have not found that your expectations for college-level work have been met, or you do not see the relevance of your coursework, you may not feel as satisfied or "well" in this area.

When students recognize a disconnect between their coursework and their intellectual expectations, they may consider making some changes to their plan. They may drop a course they originally thought they would enjoy or, in many cases, change their major to something they hadn't considered prior to beginning their coursework. This is perfectly normal and expected from most college freshmen. It is estimated that 50% of students will change their major at least once during the course of their college career.

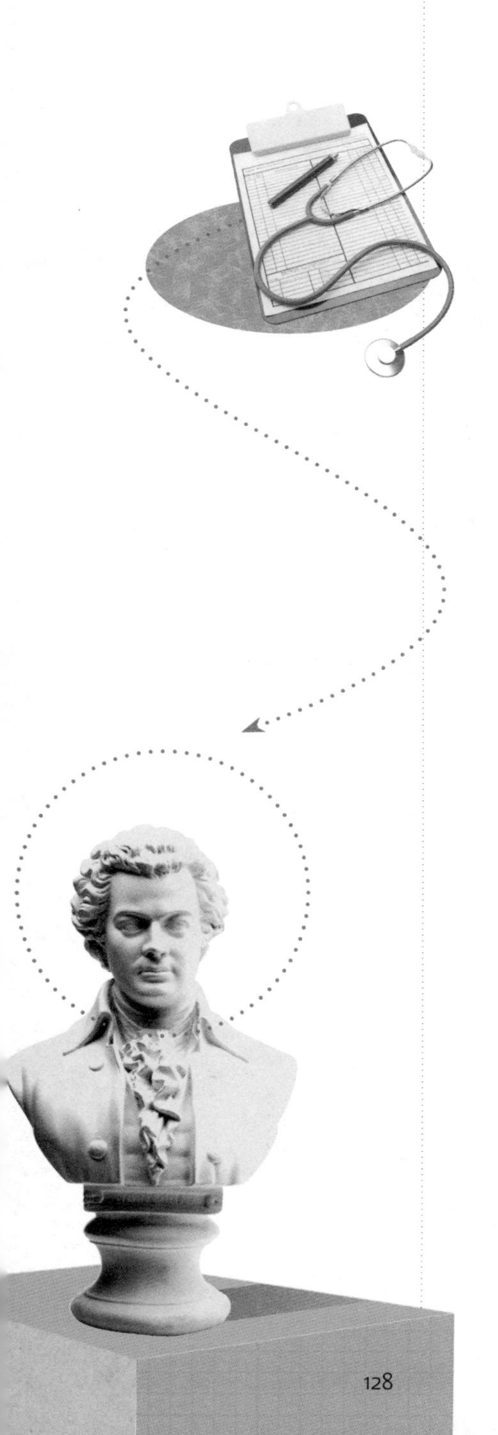

Changing your major can be a difficult decision to make. Many students come to college with a clear idea of what they want to study and how their studies will contribute to their career path. Consider this scenario:

> *Since she was a small child, Tonya had a simple answer to the question often posed to children: "What do you want to be when you grow up?" Each time, Tonya would answer quickly and definitively, "I want to be like my dad. I want to be a doctor." Tonya's father and grandfather had been physicians, so it seemed obvious that she should carry on the family tradition.*
>
> *Tonya entered college as a biology major with the distinction of being pre-med. During her first semester of college, Tonya chose to take not only biology courses, but also a history course to fulfill her humanities requirement. By midterm, Tonya was fully aware that something was not right in her academic pursuits. While Tonya did well in all of her classes, she began to realize that she did not love science—in fact, she could barely tolerate studying it.*
>
> *Tonya became involved with a pre-med club on campus. She hoped that by meeting and talking with other students dedicated to the same career goals, she would eliminate her own doubts about entering medicine. Tonya listened to speakers at those meetings and pursued job shadowing and volunteer opportunities, but soon realized she was not interested in medicine as a career. On the other hand, Tonya also joined a history reading group, which she very much enjoyed. In reading the books the group chose, Tonya realized that history, not biology or medicine, was her true academic passion. Tonya knew she was meant to be a historian, not a physician. History definitely was Tonya's calling.*

If you were a friend of Tonya's, what would you advise her to do? Many students, like Tonya, come to college with a definite idea of the career they want to pursue. It can be unsettling to find that you are not as interested in the subject as you first thought. Despite how difficult it may be to admit a change in your career plan, staying in a major and pursuing a career that you do not feel passionate about can prohibit you from feeling intellectually satisfied.

In order to be intellectually well, you need to feel challenged yet satisfied with the amount of rigor in your courses. Additionally, you need to feel confident that your coursework will, in fact, benefit your future work and prepare you for your desired career. If you are not satisfied with your major, discuss your concerns with an academic advisor or visit your career center and complete a skills and interest inventory. You will find that you are more satisfied with your intellectual path if you believe in the purpose of your work and see the connection to your future goals.

ENGAGING IN RESEARCH

Life on a college campus can be intellectually stimulating! You have the opportunity to attend lectures and presentations by scholars who are well known in their field of study; you are provided access to a library system larger and more complex than any you have experienced before; and you can engage with and learn from faculty who are not only well versed in their disciplines but actively discovering new information through research in their field. You may decide to join a faculty member in their research as a way of enhancing your academic experience and sharpening your inquiry skills. Participating in undergraduate research not only allows you to apply what you are learning in the classroom to real-world circumstances, but can also help you prepare for graduate work in your field.

Many first-year students are uncertain where to begin when it comes to undergraduate research. First, you should take some time to reflect upon your areas of interest. Once you have identified an area you would like to explore, set up an appointment to meet with a faculty member who has a shared interest. If you need help identifying a faculty mentor, you

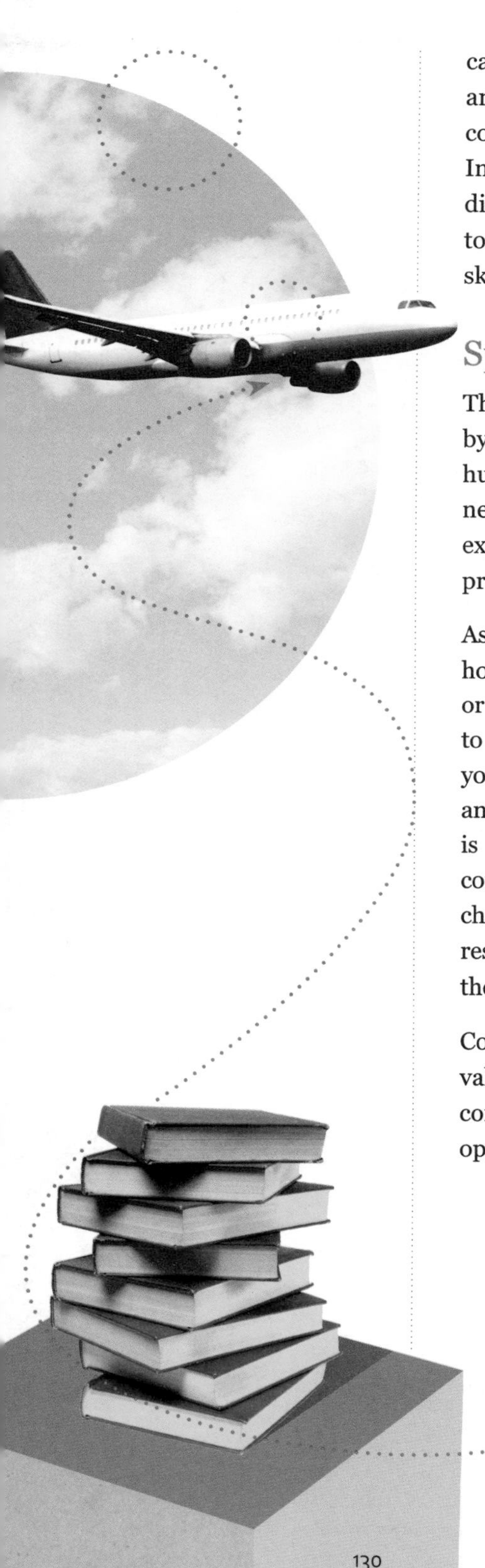

can meet with the department chair or dean to help you find an appropriate professor. You may think of research as being conducted only in a science lab with beakers and test tubes. In fact, research occurs all over a college campus, in every discipline, and participation in a research project allows you to enhance your résumé by helping you develop valuable skills like questioning, innovation, and critical thinking.

Spiritual Wellness

The final component of your overall wellness is determined by the degree to which you seek meaning and purpose in human existence. The idea of being spiritually well does not necessarily mean practicing a religion, but rather how you explore purpose and meaning of life through practices like prayer, meditation, and philosophic inquiry.

As you may have already discovered, college campuses are home to a diverse array of people. You may have a roommate or friend who is of a different religion than you. As you get to know students from various backgrounds, you may find yourself challenging the things you were raised to believe in and reconsidering the values your family instilled in you. It is perfectly normal, and also a healthy practice, for you to consider the ideas of others and how their ideas and beliefs challenge or confirm your own beliefs. It is even okay, after respectfully listening to the ideas of others, for you to challenge their beliefs and also reconsider the things you value.

College campuses are safe environments to explore your values and try new experiences. Challenge yourself to consider the ideas and practices of others with the following opportunities:

- *Attend a religious ceremony that is different than your own.*
- *Interview an international student.*
- *Attend a cultural event such as a theatrical performance, dance performance, and/or music recital.*
- *Spend a semester studying abroad.*
- *Volunteer at a community agency.*

Because of the many resources and services you have access to during your college career, now is the perfect time to try new things. As you are exploring the many facets of your wellness, don't be afraid to embrace new experiences and challenge what you have grown up believing. You may find that after participating in a new experience, you confirm your beliefs and feel more confident about your values. You may also find that you want to further explore some of the things you have learned through your interaction in these diverse communities.

Conclusion

There are many facets to your personal wellness and it can be overwhelming to consider each of these areas. Don't worry! It is not difficult to achieve wellness if you remember the key concepts of moderation, variety, and balance. Because the dimensions of the wellness wheel are interrelated, when one area is out of balance, the whole wheel is out of balance. Imagine having four tires on your car that have varying degrees of air pressure. What kind of ride are you going to have? Not a very smooth one. The same is true for your life. If your wellness wheel is out of balance, your journey through life becomes a bumpy ride. For example, if you spend all your time studying but fail to build healthy support networks of friends and family, get adequate sleep, or incorporate sufficient physical activity and a balanced diet into your daily routine, then your wellness wheel—and your life—will be unbalanced.

With all the demands you will face as a student, how can you consistently make choices that will help you to be well, maintain balance, and contribute to your academic success? Being familiar with your campus resources so you can use them is a good first step toward keeping yourself well. Your campus likely hosts many resources, most of which are free for students, to help keep you well. Resources such as the counseling center, campus ministry groups, dieticians and nutritionists, the exercise facility or gym, community service programs, and academic advisors, offer services to assist you in keeping yourself healthy.

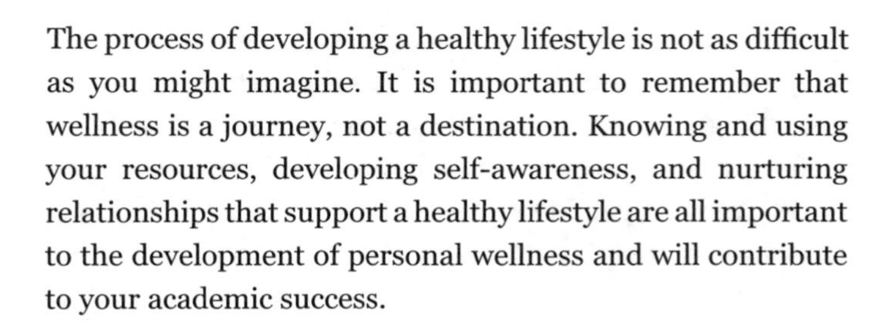

The process of developing a healthy lifestyle is not as difficult as you might imagine. It is important to remember that wellness is a journey, not a destination. Knowing and using your resources, developing self-awareness, and nurturing relationships that support a healthy lifestyle are all important to the development of personal wellness and will contribute to your academic success.

References

United States Department of Agriculture. www.mypyramid.gov

Center on Addiction and the Family, Phoenix House. Retrieved from: www.factsontap.org/index.htm

Hingson, R., Heeren, T., Winter, M., Wechsler, H. (2005). *Magnitude of alcohol-related mortality and morbidity among U.S. college students ages 18-24: Changes from 1998 to 2001.* Annual Review of Public Health, 26, 259-79; Boston University School of Public Health, Center to Prevent Alcohol Problems Among Young People, Boston, Massachusetts

Southern Illinois University, Carbondale. CORE Institute. (2006). The core alcohol and drug survey results.

Pryor, J. H., Hurtado, S., Saenz, V. B., Santos, J. L., & Korn, W. S. (2007). *The American freshman: Forty year trends.* Los Angeles: Higher Education Research Institute, University of California Los Angeles.

Start Right

Get Off to a Good Start in College

Now that you are settled in at college, make sure you get off to the right start. How are you feeling about this transition?

It is perfectly normal to have lots of feelings and emotions circling in your head right now. Not to worry, change can be both exciting and scary at the same time. You are embarking on a journey of self-discovery that will lead you toward learning new skills, making new friends, and stretching your mind, heart, and soul as you progress toward completing your degree. So, start right!

- ***Attend all of your classes.***
- ***Get to know your professors.***
- ***Work to improve your study skills.***
- ***Don't forget to meet with your academic advisor from time to time.***
- ***Interview students who have been successful. Find out what they have done in their college experience to "get on the right track."***
- ***Take notes, ask questions, and get clarification if you're confused.***
- ***Ask advisors and professors what they have noted about students who are successful in their college journey.***

Enjoy the journey!

Record IMPORTANT EVENTS

sunday	monday
	1 Ramadan
7	8
14	15
21	22
28	29

Act Can't get it all done? Prioritize!

tuesday	wednesday	thursday	friday	saturday
2	3	4	5	6
9	10	11	12	13
16	17	18	19	20
23	24	25	26	27
30	31 Eid al-Fitr			

Think THIS WEEK'S GOALS, PROJECTS, IDEAS

Record ASSIGNMENTS & TESTS

Get Organized Immediately

Create a log for all classwork and papers on a master calendar at the beginning of each term.

Keep electronic version and hard-copy versions. Start your day by reviewing this important information and determining your schedule. Plan your week of tasks in advance. Display your calendars where you will see them, and update them daily.

Act PLAN MY PRIORITIES

a.m. p.m.

1 monday

Ramadan

2 tuesday

3 wednesday

4 thursday

5 friday

6 saturday

7 sunday

Check REVIEW & REFLECT

✓ Did I achieve my weekly goals? → What didn't get accomplished?

Think THIS WEEK'S GOALS, PROJECTS, IDEAS

Record ASSIGNMENTS & TESTS

WELCOME

Explore Dorm Options

Explore your options in dormitory accommodations. Special themes are common, such as foreign language, international, healthy lifestyles, single-sex, and so on.

Decide whether you would enjoy living with students of similar interests. Plan ahead and apply early for such opportunities.

Act PLAN MY PRIORITIES

a.m. p.m.

8 monday

9 tuesday

10 wednesday

11 thursday

12 friday

13 saturday

14 sunday

Check REVIEW & REFLECT

✓ Did I achieve my weekly goals? → What didn't get accomplished?

Think THIS WEEK'S GOALS, PROJECTS, IDEAS

Record ASSIGNMENTS & TESTS

Keep Syllabi and Course Documents

Keep course syllabi and notes organized and at hand.

Not only will you use the information for the course, you may need it during advising sessions, if you apply to transfer credits to another college, or when you have an interview for an internship or job. At the end of each week for each course, summarize the critical information; the notes will be useful for later exams, licensure tests, and so on.

Act PLAN MY PRIORITIES

a.m. ✓ →

p.m. ✓ →

15 monday

16 tuesday

17 wednesday

18 thursday

19 friday

20 saturday

21 sunday

Check REVIEW & REFLECT ✓ Did I achieve my weekly goals? → What didn't get accomplished?

Think THIS WEEK'S GOALS, PROJECTS, IDEAS

Record ASSIGNMENTS & TESTS

Locate Multiple Study Areas

Locate multiple study areas on and near campus.

Make a master list of places to work undisturbed; ask more experienced students for suggestions. Use the areas even for short periods. Avoid studying where your friends congregate or in locations that have other built-in distractions. Form the habit of studying in the library, for instance, rather than in your dorm room.

Act PLAN MY PRIORITIES a.m. p.m.

22 monday

23 tuesday

24 wednesday

25 thursday

26 friday

27 saturday

28 sunday

Check REVIEW & REFLECT ✓ Did I achieve my weekly goals? → What didn't get accomplished?

Create a Daily Schedule

Developing a daily schedule is crucial to being an effective student and meeting all of the competing demands of your college experience.

After your first day of classes, immediately develop a calendar that clearly details all important dates for the semester:

1. *Write down all class sessions, meetings, and labs with specific dates and times.*
2. *Next write down every assignment for the entire semester with specific due dates.*
3. *Note when you should begin each assignment. Start each one well ahead of due dates.*
4. *Mark all tests and assessments, and make note of when you should start studying for them.*
5. *Double check your entries; review all dates to make certain they are accurate.*
6. *Proofread your work; run grammar and spell checks. Exchange your work with a reliable peer, or use the resources in your school's writing center to improve your work.*
7. *Save all your work in a secure location, both electronically and hard copy. Do not delete your work after submitting it to your professor.*
8. *Develop an ongoing portfolio of your best work. This will allow you to see the progression of your coursework. It can also be invaluable when applying for a major, scholastic honor, and so on.*

After you have all of the above carefully recorded in your planner, make a schedule for every day of the week. It is also helpful to have a weekly and monthly schedule. Be serious about using a calendar to organize yourself and your work.

Record IMPORTANT EVENTS

sunday	monday
4	5 Labor Day
11 Patriot Day	12
18	19
25	26

Act Can't get it all done? Prioritize!

SEPTEMBER 2011

tuesday	wednesday	thursday	friday	saturday
		1	2	3
6	7	8	9	10
13	14	15	16	17
20	21	22	23	24
27	28	29 Rosh Hashanah	30	

Think THIS WEEK'S GOALS, PROJECTS, IDEAS

Record ASSIGNMENTS & TESTS

Learn Where to Find Help in Each Course

Tutoring and academic support services can greatly enhance your learning.

Early in the term, find out if your professor offers review times, supervises graduate teaching assistants who lead small sessions, or recommends student tutors who know the course material. Don't wait until you are struggling in class or are approaching a test—use the available support regularly. All students, even those who are not having trouble in a class, can benefit from these resources.

Act PLAN MY PRIORITIES

a.m. p.m.

29 monday
AUG.

30 tuesday
AUG.

31 wednesday
AUG.
Eid al-Fitr

1 thursday

2 friday

3 saturday

4 sunday

Check REVIEW & REFLECT

✓ Did I achieve my weekly goals? → What didn't get accomplished?

Think THIS WEEK'S GOALS, PROJECTS, IDEAS

Record ASSIGNMENTS & TESTS

Know Your Professors

They are key to your learning and college success.

During each first class of the term, record each professor's office location and hours, e-mail address, and phone number. Also get the names and contact information of at least two students in each class so you can ask for clarification of information, assignment questions and collaborations, notes for classes you missed, and so on. Organize this information so that it is easily accessible, and save it in multiple locations.

Act PLAN MY PRIORITIES

a.m.

p.m.

5 monday

Labor Day

6 tuesday

7 wednesday

8 thursday

9 friday

10 saturday

11 sunday

Patriot Day

Check REVIEW & REFLECT

✓ Did I achieve my weekly goals? → What didn't get accomplished?

Think THIS WEEK'S GOALS, PROJECTS, IDEAS

Record ASSIGNMENTS & TESTS

Create a Daily Schedule

Make a list of each day's activities: classes, individual study time, study group meetings, extracurricular activities and events, recreation, and unscheduled time.

Try to stick to your schedule. Developing a daily schedule is the key to time management, and effective time management is critical to success in the university environment.

Act PLAN MY PRIORITIES a.m. p.m.

12 monday

13 tuesday

14 wednesday

15 thursday

16 friday

17 saturday

18 sunday

Check REVIEW & REFLECT ✓ Did I achieve my weekly goals? → What didn't get accomplished?

Think THIS WEEK'S GOALS, PROJECTS, IDEAS

Record ASSIGNMENTS & TESTS

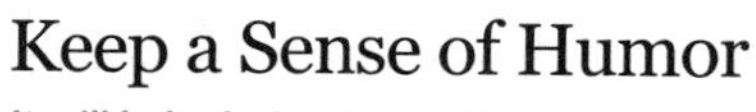

Keep a Sense of Humor

It will help during trying times.

Have within reach several things that make you laugh, so that you can relieve stress and improve your mood when necessary. Know that you will have "down" times, so think ahead.

Act PLAN MY PRIORITIES

a.m. ✓→

p.m. ✓→

19 monday

20 tuesday

21 wednesday

22 thursday

23 friday

24 saturday

25 sunday

Check REVIEW & REFLECT

✓ Did I achieve my weekly goals? → What didn't get accomplished?

Think THIS WEEK'S GOALS, PROJECTS, IDEAS

Record ASSIGNMENTS & TESTS

Get to Know the Library

Tour every campus library and find out how each one can enhance your academic success.

In your first week of classes each term, ask about resources that relate to your classes. Find out which materials are available through interlibrary loans. Meet the reference librarians; their job is to assist you with your research needs.

Act PLAN MY PRIORITIES a.m. p.m.

26 monday

27 tuesday

28 wednesday

29 thursday

Rosh Hashanah

30 friday

1 saturday
OCT.

2 sunday
OCT.

Check REVIEW & REFLECT ✓ Did I achieve my weekly goals? → What didn't get accomplished?

Study Daily for Each Class

Devote 2-3 hours of concentrated study daily for each hour spent in class with your professor.

Look at the syllabus or any related online information for each class period. Read all suggested and optional readings and resource materials prior to attending class. As you study, take good notes. Identify critical concepts and important ideas, and develop questions and comments you may wish to incorporate into the class session. Be sure to review these major points prior to the beginning of the next class:

* ***Spend some time studying with peers in your class, forming a work-focused study group.***
* ***Compare information regarding big ideas and critical concepts, and formulate critical-thinking questions based on these important concepts.***
* ***Spend time reflecting about the material you have studied.***
* ***Make connections to prior learning as well as your life and the world around you.***
* ***Keep up with your studies on a daily basis—it is important not to procrastinate.***
* ***Don't cram! Use a consistent, methodical approach to studying and integrating course material to better support your learning.***

Studying daily is important; it takes both time and effort. Preparation before class and review after class are important for your learning and retention of course material.

Act Can't get it all done? Prioritize!

OCTOBER 2011

tuesday	wednesday	thursday	friday	saturday
				1
4	5	6	7	8 Yom Kippur
11	12	13	14	15
18	19	20	21	22
25	26 Diwali	27	28	29

Check Did you finish your important tasks and goals?

Think THIS WEEK'S GOALS, PROJECTS, IDEAS

Record ASSIGNMENTS & TESTS

Inquire about Honors Programs

Many opportunities are available.

Although many programs are offered only to entering students, some are available to enrolled students in their first or second year. Many honors programs provide wonderful opportunities for qualified students, offering small class sizes, specialized seminars, tour opportunities, cultural options, faculty mentorship, registration priority, and so on.

Act PLAN MY PRIORITIES — a.m. / p.m.

3 monday

4 tuesday

5 wednesday

6 thursday

7 friday

8 saturday — Yom Kippur

9 sunday

Check REVIEW & REFLECT ✓ Did I achieve my weekly goals? → What didn't get accomplished?

Think THIS WEEK'S GOALS, PROJECTS, IDEAS

Record ASSIGNMENTS & TESTS

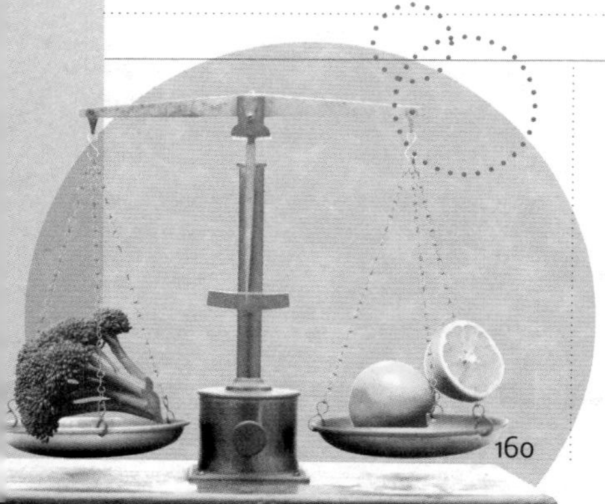

Eat Well

Make sure your diet is balanced and nutritious.

Your body needs proper nourishment to fuel daily activities. Don't skip any meals, especially breakfast. Keep nonperishable and nutritious snacks on hand for intensive study times, so that you will be able to avoid the temptation to eat junk food. Drink water plenty of times so you can avoid the unnecessary sugars.

Act PLAN MY PRIORITIES

a.m. ✓ →

p.m. ✓ →

10 monday

Columbus Day

11 tuesday

12 wednesday

13 thursday

14 friday

15 saturday

16 sunday

Check REVIEW & REFLECT ✓ Did I achieve my weekly goals? → What didn't get accomplished?

Think THIS WEEK'S GOALS, PROJECTS, IDEAS

Record ASSIGNMENTS & TESTS

Study Daily for Each Class

Devote 2-3 hours of concentrated study for each hour spent in class.

Look at the syllabus and related information for each class period. Go over class readings and material before each class, making study notes and developing questions and comments for the session. After each class, note the big ideas, then include your notes in your preclass review. Daily studying and frequent review will help you retain information.

Act PLAN MY PRIORITIES a.m. p.m.

17 monday

18 tuesday

19 wednesday

20 thursday

21 friday

22 saturday

23 sunday

Check REVIEW & REFLECT ✓ Did I achieve my weekly goals? → What didn't get accomplished?

Think THIS WEEK'S GOALS, PROJECTS, IDEAS

Record ASSIGNMENTS & TESTS

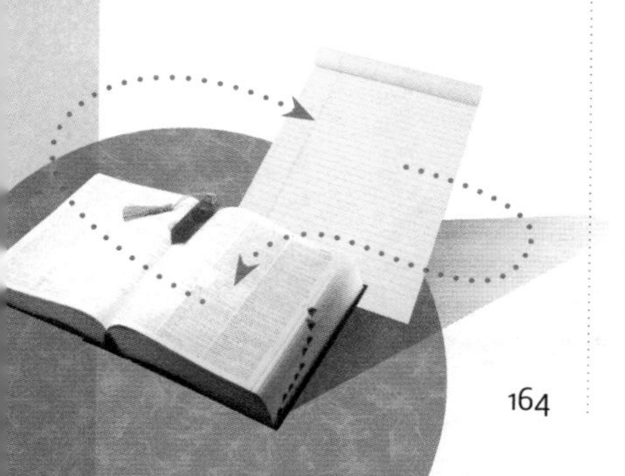

Acknowledge Information Sources

Carefully credit and acknowledge all sources of information used in your academic work.

Plagiarism is a problem on most college campuses, and professors have effective ways of rooting it out. Make an appointment with a librarian or a staff member at the writing center if you are not sure how to credit sources in your papers, presentations, and other work.

Act PLAN MY PRIORITIES

a.m. p.m.

24 monday

25 tuesday

26 wednesday

Diwali

27 thursday

28 friday

29 saturday

30 sunday

Check REVIEW & REFLECT ✓ Did I achieve my weekly goals? → What didn't get accomplished?

Go to All Classes

Don't cut classes even if there is not an attendance policy stated on the syllabus or by the professor.

Assume the professor knows a great deal more than you do about the subject matter, and that you will benefit from each class you attend. Don't rely on notes from your peers or their summary of class events.

* ***Divide your tuition by the number of class sessions per semester and see what you are losing monetarily when you skip class.***
* ***Schedule your classes for times that work best for you. For example, if you stay up late at night studying, avoid scheduling an early-morning class.***

Class attendance and assignments/work need to be your first priority. It is easy to make excuses for skipping classes, especially in larger lecture halls. And if you skip classes you will miss important content.

Furthermore, you will not know about important announcements and perhaps class-schedule changes. You may miss critical information regarding assignments, projects, and exams. You could also miss out on supports, such as tutorials, that may be offered to assist you.

Professors spend a great deal of time developing their expertise; take full advantage of their knowledge and experience. Keep in mind your ultimate goal for college—to get a very good education.

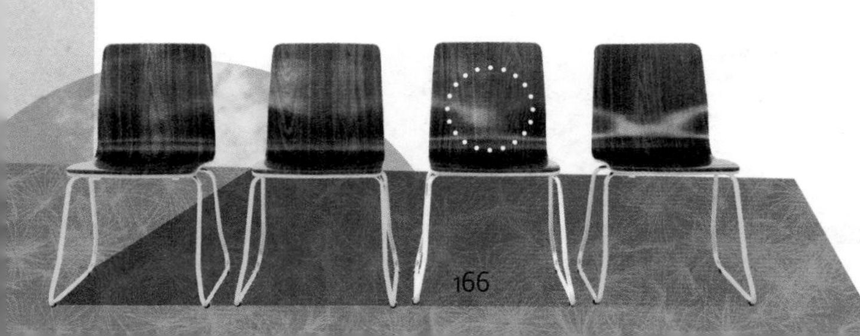

Record IMPORTANT EVENTS

sunday	monday
6	7 Eid al-Adha
13	14
20	21
27 Muharram	28

Act Can't get it all done? Prioritize!

NOVEMBER 2011

tuesday	wednesday	thursday	friday	saturday
1	2	3	4	5
8	9	10	11 Veterans Day	12
15	16	17	18	19
22	23	24 Thanksgiving Day	25	26
29	30			

Check Did you finish your important tasks and goals?

Think THIS WEEK'S GOALS, PROJECTS, IDEAS

Record ASSIGNMENTS & TESTS

Monitor Your GPA

Don't wait until the end of the term to check on your grade status.

Always know how you are doing in each course, and communicate with your professors as soon as issues arise. If you feel your grade is inaccurate, advocate for yourself and support your case with documentation and evidence.

Act PLAN MY PRIORITIES

a.m.

p.m.

31 OCT. monday

Halloween

1 tuesday

2 wednesday

3 thursday

4 friday

5 saturday

6 sunday

Check REVIEW & REFLECT

✓ Did I achieve my weekly goals? → What didn't get accomplished?

Think THIS WEEK'S GOALS, PROJECTS, IDEAS

Record ASSIGNMENTS & TESTS

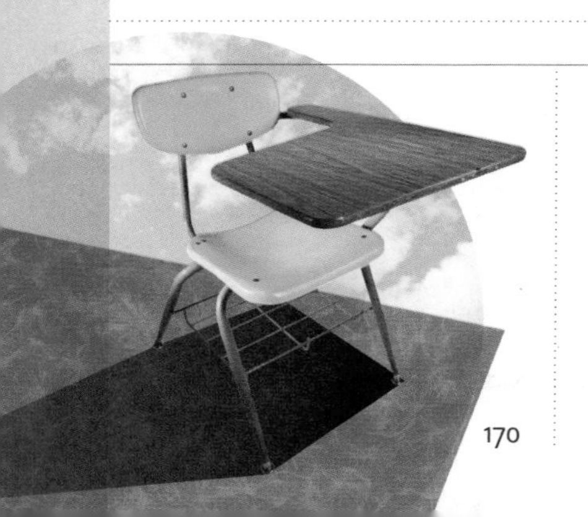

Attend All Classes

Don't cut classes, even if there is no penalty for doing so.

Assume that the professor knows a great deal more than you do about the subject matter and that you will benefit from each class you attend. Don't rely on notes or summaries from your peers. You have paid for your classes, so missing class is wasting money. Try to schedule your classes at times when you are likely to attend them.

Act PLAN MY PRIORITIES | a.m. | p.m.

7 monday — Eid al-Adha

8 tuesday

9 wednesday

10 thursday

11 friday — Veterans Day

12 saturday

13 sunday

Check REVIEW & REFLECT ✓ Did I achieve my weekly goals? → What didn't get accomplished?

Think THIS WEEK'S GOALS, PROJECTS, IDEAS

Record ASSIGNMENTS & TESTS

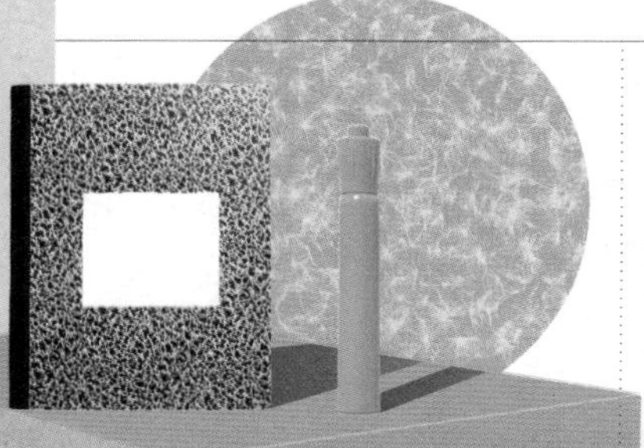

Join Study Groups

Join or organize study groups and explore possibilities related to learning communities.

On the first day of class, get names, e-mail addresses, and phone numbers of peers you may wish to work with collaboratively. Organize this information to be easily accessible. Set periodic small-group study times and divide the workload (for example, summarizing text chapters) consistently throughout the term. Make certain all members of the group contribute equally.

Act PLAN MY PRIORITIES

a.m.

p.m.

14 monday

15 tuesday

16 wednesday

17 thursday

18 friday

19 saturday

20 sunday

Check REVIEW & REFLECT ✓ Did I achieve my weekly goals? → What didn't get accomplished?

Think THIS WEEK'S GOALS, PROJECTS, IDEAS

Record ASSIGNMENTS & TESTS

zzzzzzzzzzzzzzzzzzzzzzzz

Get Enough Sleep

Get plenty of sleep to function well in classes and during your study time; many college students do not.

If your dorm, like many, is noisy at night, you may need to use earplugs and eye shades or play soothing music through headphones so you can sleep. Discuss with your roommate(s) your sleeping patterns and how you can support each other to get the maximum amount of rest. Plan for adequate sleep, and put the hours on your daily planner.

Act PLAN MY PRIORITIES

a.m. ✓ →

p.m. ✓ →

21 monday

22 tuesday

23 wednesday

24 thursday

Thanksgiving Day

25 friday

26 saturday

27 sunday

Muharram

Check REVIEW & REFLECT

✓ Did I achieve my weekly goals? → What didn't get accomplished?

Develop a Plan of Action

Devise a personal plan of action for each course every semester.

Formulate detailed and specific course goals and an action plan of how you will accomplish each goal. Include a specific timeline for completion of each goal. Make certain your plan is clearly tied to course requirements, assignments, examinations, and deadlines.

All of this information needs to be included as part of your comprehensive plan. Put this information in columns and headings in a well-organized fashion and refer to it daily. You may choose headings such as: Course Goal 1.1; Objectives to Meet; Steps to Completion; Timeline for Meeting Goal; Completion of Goal, etc.

Thorough planning is an important key to your academic success—be thoughtful about your goals and be specific in your goal-setting.

* ***Students who develop action plans typically are more focused and know their goals.***
* ***It is difficult to achieve goals that have not been formulated!***
* ***As you develop a plan of action, think about the most important learning goals for each course.***
* ***What are your specific learning goals and what is your timeline for completion?***

You may benefit from setting monthly goals for each class. Or, perhaps you wish to set weekly or chapter goals. Whichever way you determine to format your plan, you are likely to achieve far more by identifying your goals.

Record IMPORTANT EVENTS

sunday	monday
4	5
11	12
18	19
25 Christmas Day	26 Kwanzaa

Act Can't get it all done? Prioritize!

DECEMBER 2011

tuesday	wednesday	thursday	friday	saturday
		1	2	3
6	7	8	9	10
13	14	15	16	17
20	21 Hanukkah	22	23	24
27	28	29	30	31

Check Did you finish your important tasks and goals?

Think THIS WEEK'S GOALS, PROJECTS, IDEAS

Record ASSIGNMENTS & TESTS

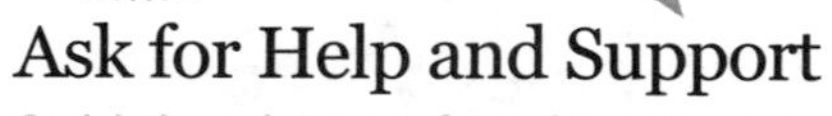

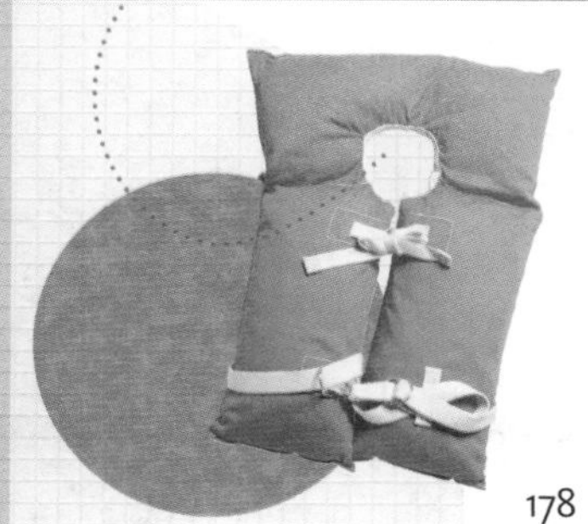

Ask for Help and Support

Seek help and support from the many services on campus.

Depression, academic problems, career questions, housing issues, and many other areas of concern are addressed by various campus services. Become knowledgeable about what is available to you and how to access the services; most campuses run orientations and events to help students find out what is offered.

Act PLAN MY PRIORITIES

a.m.

p.m.

28 monday
NOV.

29 tuesday
NOV.

30 wednesday
NOV.

1 thursday

2 friday

3 saturday

4 sunday

Check REVIEW & REFLECT

✓ Did I achieve my weekly goals? → What didn't get accomplished?

Record ASSIGNMENTS & TESTS

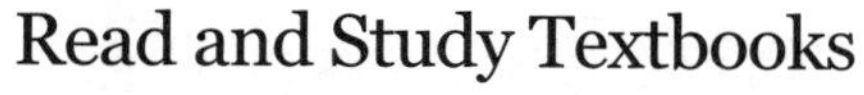

Read and Study Textbooks

Read and study textbooks and other readings for each course.

Professors have good reasons for their assignments. Come to class prepared with notes and questions. As a rule of thumb, prepare three questions or thoughtful comments prior to each class. Reflect on the application of the course material to the world outside the classroom.

Act PLAN MY PRIORITIES | a.m. | p.m.

5 monday

6 tuesday

7 wednesday

8 thursday

9 friday

10 saturday

11 sunday

Check REVIEW & REFLECT ✓ Did I achieve my weekly goals? → What didn't get accomplished?

Think THIS WEEK'S GOALS, PROJECTS, IDEAS

Record ASSIGNMENTS & TESTS

Take Part in Book Exchanges

You may save money and recycle good textbooks.

Shop early, since used books often sell out. Comparison-shop campus bookstores and online merchants, or consider buying a textbook from someone who previously took the course. Make certain the textbook is still being used for the course and that you have the most recent edition, if necessary.

Act PLAN MY PRIORITIES a.m. ✓→ p.m. ✓→

12 monday

13 tuesday

14 wednesday

15 thursday

16 friday

17 saturday

18 sunday

Check REVIEW & REFLECT ✓ Did I achieve my weekly goals? → What didn't get accomplished?

Think THIS WEEK'S GOALS, PROJECTS, IDEAS

Record ASSIGNMENTS & TESTS

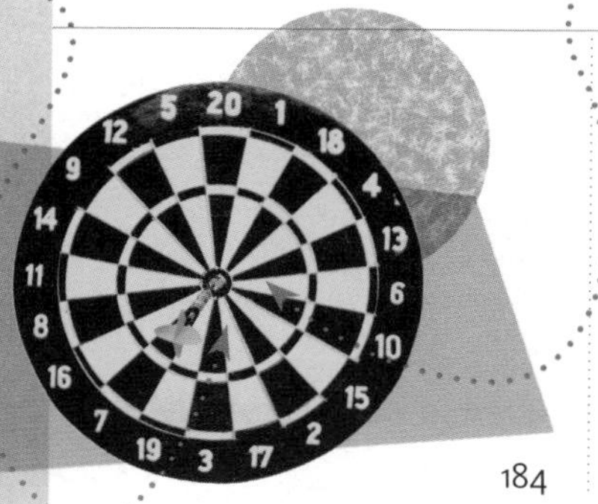

Develop a Personal Plan of Action

Develop a personal plan of action for each course you take.

Formulate detailed and specific course goals, and decide how and when you will reach each goal. Make certain your plan is comprehensive and clearly tied to course requirements, assignments, examinations, and deadlines. Make a chart of the information and refer to it daily. Sample headings might include Course Goal; Objectives to Meet; Steps to Completion; Timeline; and so on. Organize the plan of action in a way that works for you.

DECEMBER 2011

Act PLAN MY PRIORITIES

a.m. p.m.

19 monday

20 tuesday

21 wednesday

Hanukkah

22 thursday

23 friday

24 saturday

25 sunday

Christmas Day

Check REVIEW & REFLECT ✓ Did I achieve my weekly goals? → What didn't get accomplished?

Think THIS WEEK'S GOALS, PROJECTS, IDEAS

Record ASSIGNMENTS & TESTS

Assemble a Toolkit

Organize pens, a stapler, tape, clips, PDA, iPod, computer materials, notebooks, and related materials so you will not waste time locating or purchasing them.

A well-organized toolkit should enable you to be ready to work, with everything you need close at hand. Find a system to organize all equipment and materials and put things back in their proper places.

Act PLAN MY PRIORITIES

a.m.

p.m.

26 monday

Kwanzaa

27 tuesday

28 wednesday

29 thursday

30 friday

31 saturday

1 JAN. sunday

New Year's Day

Check REVIEW & REFLECT

✓ Did I achieve my weekly goals? → What didn't get accomplished?

Locate Academic Support Services

Know and locate all academic support services and resources before you start classes.

- ***Many schools have a variety of programs that support and enhance the success of students in their academic coursework. Ask early about the services provided and the location of each one of these resources. Go early and often to learn about how each resource can assist you in your success.***
- ***Review these services online and go in person to the location of each support service. Talk with the staff personnel and know how to access and utilize each service.***
- ***Examples of resources and services are: organized sessions to review material prior to midterm and final exams, time-management workshops, writing center assistance and support, counseling center.***

Your tuition and fees are paying for academic support services to enhance your success in college. If you don't utilize, or underutilize, these services and supports, You're wasting money by using them sparingly or not at all.

Develop a plan to use these support services. Start by identifying and developing a list of all such services.

- ***Include specific contact information and lead time needed, if any. For example, does the writing center have electronic or e-mail submissions? If you submit assignments, how much lead time is required?***
- ***Compose a detailed chart of all academic support services.***
- ***Highlight those support services you need to utilize more or for the first time.***

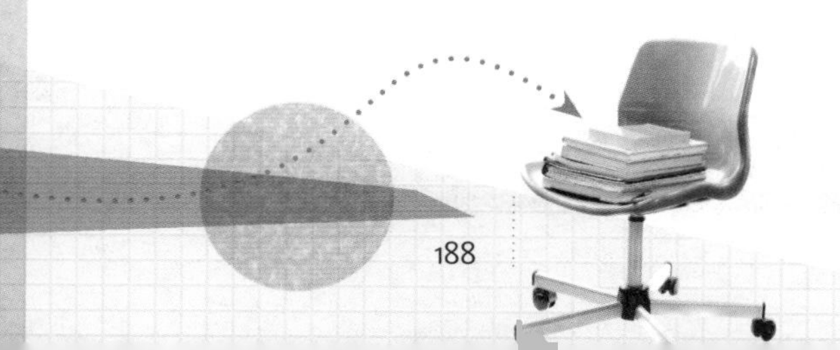

Record IMPORTANT EVENTS

sunday	monday
1 New Year's Day	2
8	9
15	16 Martin Luther King, Jr. Day
22	23 Chinese New Year
29	30

Act Can't get it all done? Prioritize!

JANUARY 2012

tuesday	wednesday	thursday	friday	saturday
3	4	5	6	7
10	11	12	13	14
17	18	19	20	21
24	25	26	27	28
31				

Check Did you finish your important tasks and goals?

Record ASSIGNMENTS & TESTS

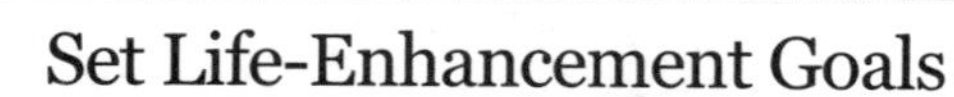

Set Life-Enhancement Goals

Set at least one life-enhancement goal for each term.

For example, you may choose to work on oral communication or presentation skills. Take advantage of opportunities to strengthen and develop your selected goal. Ask trusted faculty, program advisors, and peers to suggest strategies that will help you reach your goal. Evaluate your progress frequently throughout the term, and seek opportunities every day to work toward your goal.

Act PLAN MY PRIORITIES a.m. p.m.

2 monday

3 tuesday

4 wednesday

5 thursday

6 friday

7 saturday

8 sunday

Check REVIEW & REFLECT ✓ Did I achieve my weekly goals? → What didn't get accomplished?

Think THIS WEEK'S GOALS, PROJECTS, IDEAS

Record ASSIGNMENTS & TESTS

Work Ahead

Work ahead, pacing yourself and spreading your workload.

Clearly outline all work on a calendar or planner. Don't procrastinate: You'll find yourself working frantically and below your potential, and your grades will suffer. Take time to read and review your work several times before completing your final version. With every read and edit, your work should show improvement. Seek feedback from skillful peers or the campus writing center.

Act PLAN MY PRIORITIES

a.m. ✓ →

p.m. ✓ →

9 monday

10 tuesday

11 wednesday

12 thursday

13 friday

14 saturday

15 sunday

Check REVIEW & REFLECT

✓ Did I achieve my weekly goals? → What didn't get accomplished?

Think THIS WEEK'S GOALS, PROJECTS, IDEAS

Record ASSIGNMENTS & TESTS

Find the Campus Academic Support Resources

Before classes start, find the academic support services and resources.

Most schools have a variety of programs that support and enhance the academic success of students. Review online descriptions of the services, and visit their facilities. Talk with the staff and find out how to use the resources. Examples of such resources include time-management workshops, writing centers, counseling centers, and organized review sessions for specific courses.

Act PLAN MY PRIORITIES

a.m.

p.m.

16 monday

Martin Luther King, Jr. Day

17 tuesday

18 wednesday

19 thursday

20 friday

21 saturday

22 sunday

Check REVIEW & REFLECT

✓ Did I achieve my weekly goals? → What didn't get accomplished?

Think THIS WEEK'S GOALS, PROJECTS, IDEAS

Record ASSIGNMENTS & TESTS

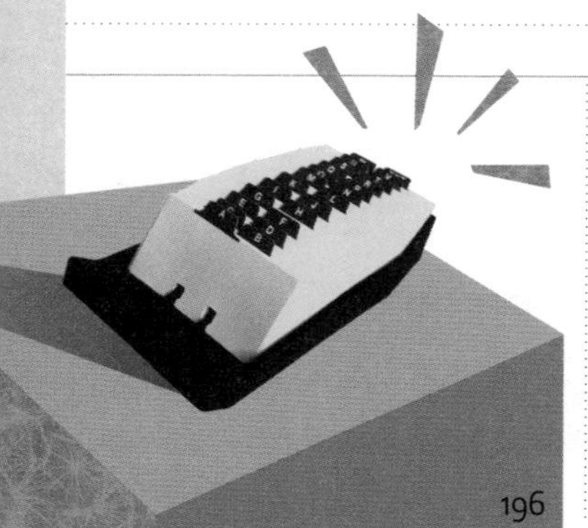

Develop a Campus-Based Support System

Compile a list of friends, advisors, faculty, and staff to whom you can turn for guidance and assistance.

Write down the contact information for every person on your list, and ask if you can call or e-mail them as the need arises. Make note of how each person might support you and how you might access his or her expertise or knowledge. Offer to assist your peers.

Act PLAN MY PRIORITIES

a.m. ✓ →

p.m. ✓ →

23 monday

Chinese New Year

24 tuesday

25 wednesday

26 thursday

27 friday

28 saturday

29 sunday

Check REVIEW & REFLECT

✓ Did I achieve my weekly goals? → What didn't get accomplished?

Engage in Extracurricular Activities

Carefully select several extracurricular activities to get involved with on your campus for each semester.

* *Start by reviewing all of the options for class activities. You should be able to find much of this information online or at your student government offices.*
* *Look for contact persons included with this basic informationand seek them out.*
* *Choose extracurricular activities that interest you and with which you have some experience, as well as others that will stretch your growth in new areas and interests. Consider carefully choosing one activity that is familiar and another that is unfamiliar so you will learn new skills and abilities.*
* *Ask if you can attend or audit a meeting to see if the activities interest you.*
* *Try many different types of activities, focusing in on a few that are of the most interest over time. Try arts, volunteering, student government, journalism and so on—all the major spheres, which gives you exposure, skills, and versatility no matter what you do as a career.*
* *Ideally, try one new activity each semester or every other semester.*
* *Assess the relative benefits of various organizations related to your personal and career goals.*
* *Use the extracurricular activities to meet new people.*

Record IMPORTANT EVENTS

sunday	monday
5	6
12	13
19	20 Presidents' Day
26	27

Act Can't get it all done? Prioritize!

FEBRUARY 2012

tuesday	wednesday	thursday	friday	saturday
	1	2	3	4
7	8	9	10	11
14 Valentine's Day	15	16	17	18
21	22	23	24	25
28	29			

Check Did you finish your important tasks and goals?

Think THIS WEEK'S GOALS, PROJECTS, IDEAS

Record ASSIGNMENTS & TESTS

Set Technology Goals

For each term, identify products and services that you will need to learn to use in your academic and extracurricular work.

Regularly read campus technology bulletins to stay up to date, and take advantage of the offerings of campus technology services. Find out how to obtain available discounts on technology products through the university.

Act PLAN MY PRIORITIES

a.m. p.m.

30 monday
JAN.

31 tuesday
JAN.

1 wednesday

2 thursday

3 friday

4 saturday

5 sunday

Check REVIEW & REFLECT

✓ Did I achieve my weekly goals? → What didn't get accomplished?

Record ASSIGNMENTS & TESTS

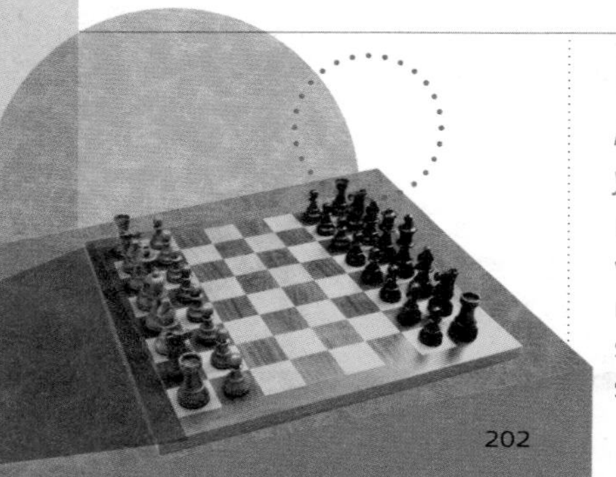

Engage in Extracurricular Activities

Extracurricular activities are important for your learning as well as for your assimilation into the college setting.

Participate in an activity each term. Choose activities that interest you and with which you have some experience, but also try others that will help you grow in new areas. Spheres of activity may include the arts, community organizations, student government, intramural sports, and clubs. You will gain experience, skills, and versatility that will benefit you no matter what career you pursue.

Act PLAN MY PRIORITIES

a.m. p.m.

6 monday

7 tuesday

8 wednesday

9 thursday

10 friday

11 saturday

12 sunday

Check REVIEW & REFLECT ✓ Did I achieve my weekly goals? → What didn't get accomplished?

Think THIS WEEK'S GOALS, PROJECTS, IDEAS

Record ASSIGNMENTS & TESTS

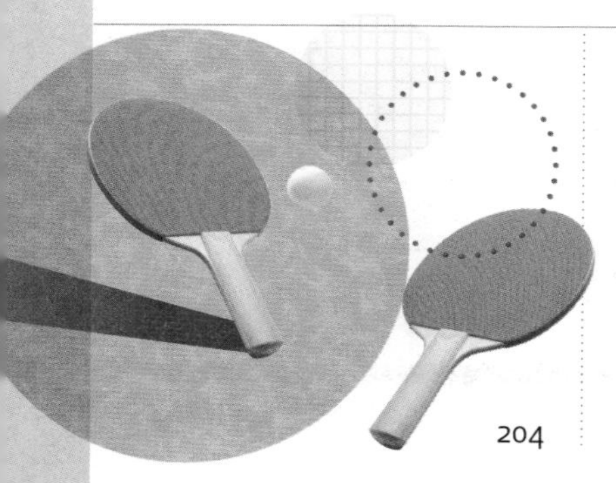

Start a New Club

Take responsibility for initiating and organizing a new program, club, activity, or group.

Ask for help, support, and assistance from knowledgeable members of the campus community. Find out whether there is funding for student groups and activities, and learn how to apply for it.

Act PLAN MY PRIORITIES a.m. p.m.

13 monday

14 tuesday Valentine's Day

15 wednesday

16 thursday

17 friday

18 saturday

19 sunday

Check REVIEW & REFLECT ✓ Did I achieve my weekly goals? → What didn't get accomplished?

Think THIS WEEK'S GOALS, PROJECTS, IDEAS

Record ASSIGNMENTS & TESTS

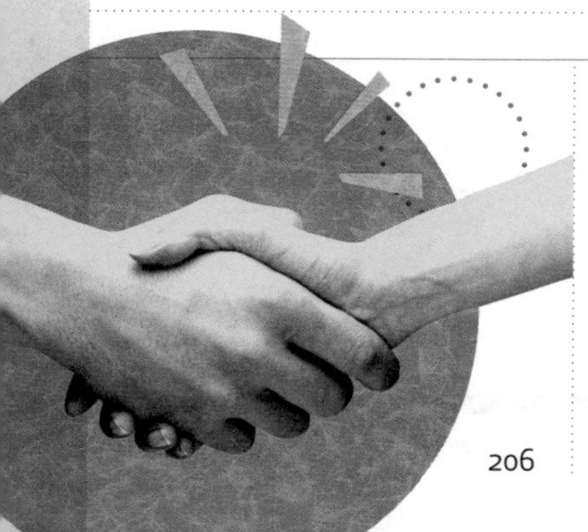

Partner with the Adults in Your Life

Partner with significant persons in your life, such as your parents, high school teachers, or other adults who have encouraged or inspired you.

Let them know how you are progressing academically, and consult them about your challenges. Consider your college years as a partnership with your parents and other valued people in your life.

Act PLAN MY PRIORITIES

a.m.

p.m.

20 monday

Presidents' Day

21 tuesday

22 wednesday

23 thursday

24 friday

25 saturday

26 sunday

Check REVIEW & REFLECT

✓ Did I achieve my weekly goals? → What didn't get accomplished?

Record IMPORTANT EVENTS

Choose Your Major Wisely

Decisions about choosing a major are frequently a source of confusion and consternation during the college years.

Investigate the variety of options for majors and minors that interest you early on. Consider a double major if you have competing and multiple interests.

Most colleges that have a liberal arts orientation allow students time to "sample" a variety of general education courses prior to beginning a major program of studies. Take advantage of this opportunity to try a variety of coursework in disciplines that interest you.

- *Talk with both faculty and students who have studied in your areas of interest.*
- *Read professional journals and join related professional clubs or organizations.*
- *Ask program advisors and faculty for their advice regarding careers and work opportunities related to your areas of interest.*
- *Consider a request to shadow an alumnus from your college/university who works in the area of interest you are considering for your major program of studies.*
- *Discuss with professors and students currently taking this major the advantages and disadvantages of this program of studies.*
- *When visiting your home over breaks and holidays, ask practitioners in your major field about job opportunities.*
- *Ask about summer internships and jobs related to your major. On-the-job experience can be very valuable following graduation.*

Act Can't get it all done? Prioritize!

MARCH 2012

tuesday	wednesday	thursday	friday	saturday
		1	2	3
6	7	8	9	10
13	14	15	16	17
20	21	22	23	24
27	28	29	30	31

Check Did you finish your important tasks and goals?

Think THIS WEEK'S GOALS, PROJECTS, IDEAS

Record ASSIGNMENTS & TESTS

Be Computer-Wise

Take advantage of college discounts and store specials.

Use care when transporting a computer from home; it may be preferable to pick up a computer locally or have one shipped to campus. If you buy a laptop, make sure it is sturdy enough to be carried back and forth, and never leave it unattended. Find out how the campus tech support can assist you when you have a problem, and if it is advisable to purchase warranties and insurance policies for your computer equipment.

Act PLAN MY PRIORITIES

a.m.

p.m.

27 monday
FEB

28 tuesday
FEB

29 wednesday
FEB

1 thursday

2 friday

3 saturday

4 sunday

Check REVIEW & REFLECT

✓ Did I achieve my weekly goals? → What didn't get accomplished?

Think THIS WEEK'S GOALS, PROJECTS, IDEAS

Record ASSIGNMENTS & TESTS

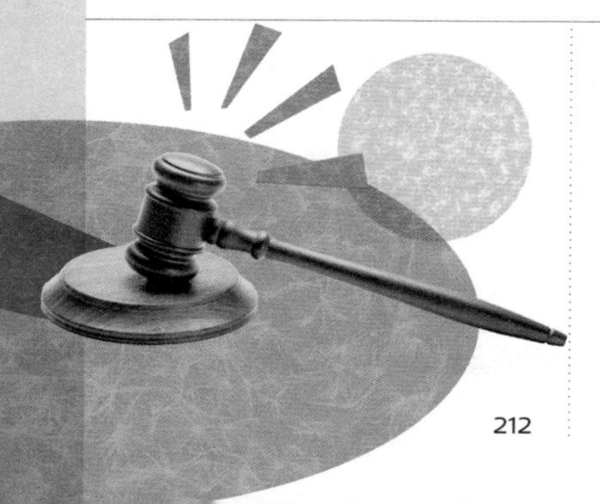

Join Professional Organizations

Choose disciplines in which you have an interest; reduced membership rates are generally available to students.

Investigate whether there is an on-campus chapter, a state or provincial chapter, or a regional chapter of each organization you might want to join. Attend conferences to network, learn about specific disciplines, and look for leadership opportunities.

Act PLAN MY PRIORITIES

a.m. p.m.

5 monday

6 tuesday

7 wednesday

8 thursday

9 friday

10 saturday

11 sunday

Check REVIEW & REFLECT ✓ Did I achieve my weekly goals? → What didn't get accomplished?

Think THIS WEEK'S GOALS, PROJECTS, IDEAS

Record ASSIGNMENTS & TESTS

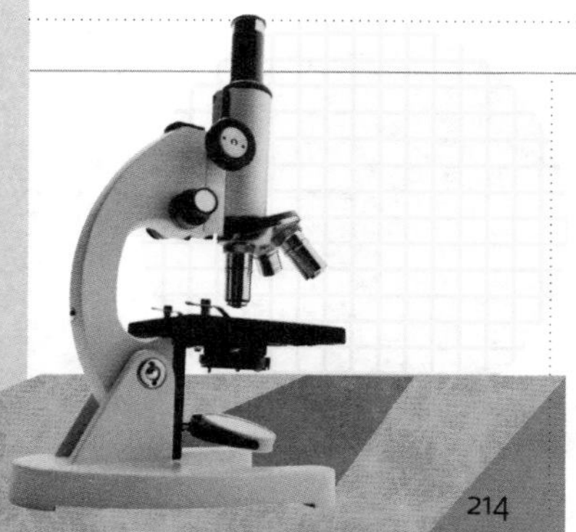

Explore Research Opportunities

Explore opportunities for undergraduate research.

Ask faculty members how you can be involved in their research projects, experiments, and professional organizations. Volunteer to assist and partner with them in their research and publication activities. College staff may also have need for research assistance. People in admissions offices, career counseling services, and student government services may conduct research related to student activities and accomplishments.

Act PLAN MY PRIORITIES

a.m. p.m.

12 monday

13 tuesday

14 wednesday

15 thursday

16 friday

17 saturday

18 sunday

Check REVIEW & REFLECT ✓ Did I achieve my weekly goals? → What didn't get accomplished?

Record ASSIGNMENTS & TESTS

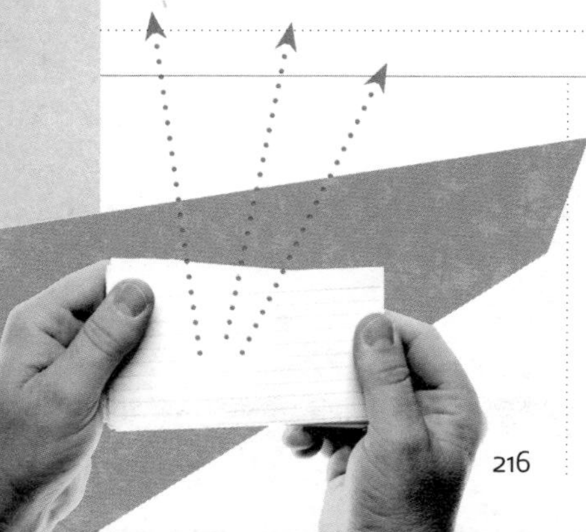

Develop Public Speaking Skills

Look for frequent, varied, and multiple opportunities to develop your public speaking skills.

Regardless of your career choice or academic trajectory, you will need to develop public speaking skills. Request feedback and suggestions from speakers, professors, and peers who are good public speakers. Consider participating in extracurricular activities that develop public communication skills, such as debate, mock trial, or theater.

Act PLAN MY PRIORITIES

a.m. p.m.

19 monday

20 tuesday

21 wednesday

22 thursday

23 friday

24 saturday

25 sunday

Check REVIEW & REFLECT

✓ Did I achieve my weekly goals? → What didn't get accomplished?

Think THIS WEEK'S GOALS, PROJECTS, IDEAS

Record ASSIGNMENTS & TESTS

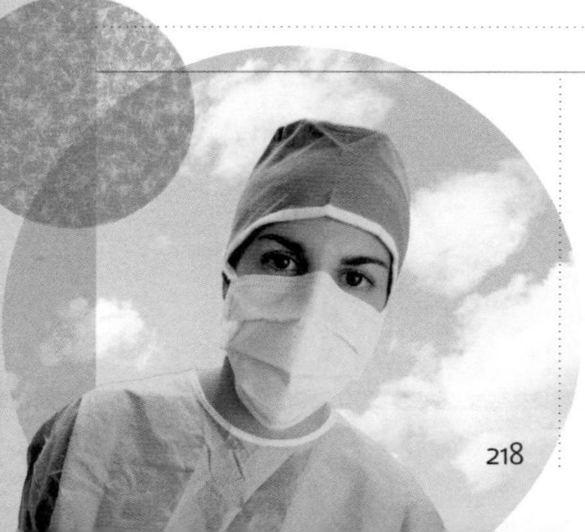

Choose Your Major Wisely

Your major will require significant effort, so it should be in a field that attracts and sustains your interest.

Investigate early the variety of options for majors and minors that interest you. Talk with both faculty and students who have studied in your areas of interest. Talk with individuals working in your discipline of interest to learn about career paths. Consider pursuing a double major if you have competing and multiple interests.

Act PLAN MY PRIORITIES

a.m. ✓ →

p.m. ✓ →

26 monday

27 tuesday

28 wednesday

29 thursday

30 friday

31 saturday

1 APR. sunday

Check REVIEW & REFLECT

✓ Did I achieve my weekly goals? → What didn't get accomplished?

Record IMPORTANT EVENTS

sunday	monday
1	2
8 Easter	9
15	16
22	23
29	30

Find Healthy Ways to Relieve Stress

Stress is inevitable in your college experience.

Even if you are a well-organized student who plans out assignments and works well in advance, you will have some "crunch" times that can become very stressful. Always be on the lookout for opportunities to reduce your stress levels:

- ***Look for running and walking partners, intramural sports teams, yoga classes, hiking opportunities/clubs, acting and theater, places to play an instrument, and so on.***
- ***Know what works for you: an outdoor run, yoga, warm tea, time alone to be quiet and reflect, a talk with a counselor, listening to soothing music, etc.***
- ***Put music on your media player that is calming; play it when needed.***

Be intentional about managing your stress; be proactive.

- ***Reflect upon the sources of your stress.***
- ***What calms you when you are stressed? Think about this carefully.***
- ***Make time in your day to incorporate ways that you can reduce and diminish your stress level.***

Who can you talk to for support and assistance?

- ***Call on friends and family as well as professional counseling services at your college during difficult and stressful times.***
- ***Keep a diary or journal page related to stress; write responses to these questions: When do you feel stressed? What are the things that stress you? What works to relax and renew you?***

Reflect and refresh yourself and your spirit.

Act Can't get it all done? Prioritize!

APRIL 2012

tuesday	wednesday	thursday	friday	saturday
3	4	5	6 Good Friday	7 Passover
10	11	12	13	14
17	18	19	20	21
24	25	26	27	28 Vesak

Check Did you finish your important tasks and goals?

Think THIS WEEK'S GOALS, PROJECTS, IDEAS

Record ASSIGNMENTS & TESTS

Explore Awards and Honors

Discover those given by your programs.

Learn early in your college career which awards and honors you might be well-positioned to apply for—campus-based, from professional organizations, and so on. Make a list of what you need to do to increase your chances of success. Ask professors, club sponsors, and previous winners what you should do to compete successfully for the award or honor.

Act PLAN MY PRIORITIES a.m. p.m.

2 monday

3 tuesday

4 wednesday

5 thursday

6 friday Good Friday

7 saturday Passover

8 sunday Easter

Check REVIEW & REFLECT ✓ Did I achieve my weekly goals? → What didn't get accomplished?

Think THIS WEEK'S GOALS, PROJECTS, IDEAS

Record ASSIGNMENTS & TESTS

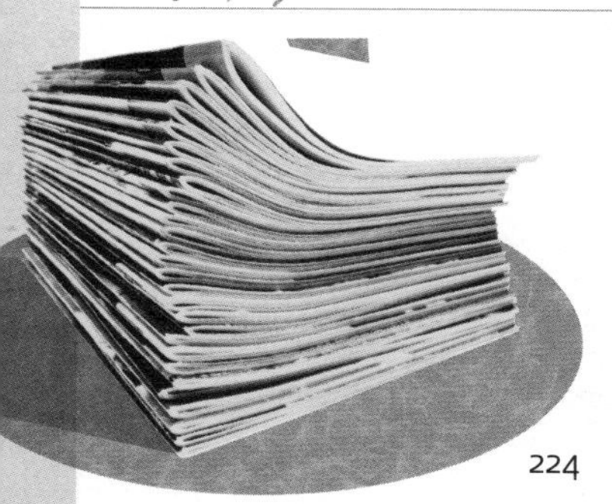

Look for Presentation and Publishing Opportunities

Explore such venues as short stories, poetry, research results, or class projects.

Be persistent; ask for help and suggestions from your professors. Ask if you can co-publish with your professor or co-present with a faculty member after you have assisted with their research. Apply to present papers at meetings of professional organizations, initially at the state or regional level. If you plan to attend graduate school, it is especially valuable to publish and present in your area of interest.

Act PLAN MY PRIORITIES

a.m. p.m.

9 monday

10 tuesday

11 wednesday

12 thursday

13 friday

14 saturday

15 sunday

Check REVIEW & REFLECT

✓ Did I achieve my weekly goals? → What didn't get accomplished?

Think THIS WEEK'S GOALS, PROJECTS, IDEAS

Record ASSIGNMENTS & TESTS

Keep Your Résumé Up to Date

Update your résumé on your computer and print it out monthly.

Regularly refine your résumé, and make notes between updates so that you don't forget important events, contributions, and accomplishments. Be sure to include all activities, courses, and extracurricular functions, as well as career goals and special interests. Highlight leadership experience. Be ready to e-mail your résumé at a moment's notice.

Act PLAN MY PRIORITIES

a.m.

p.m.

16 monday

17 tuesday

18 wednesday

19 thursday

20 friday

21 saturday

22 sunday

Check REVIEW & REFLECT

✓ Did I achieve my weekly goals? → What didn't get accomplished?

Think THIS WEEK'S GOALS, PROJECTS, IDEAS

Record ASSIGNMENTS & TESTS

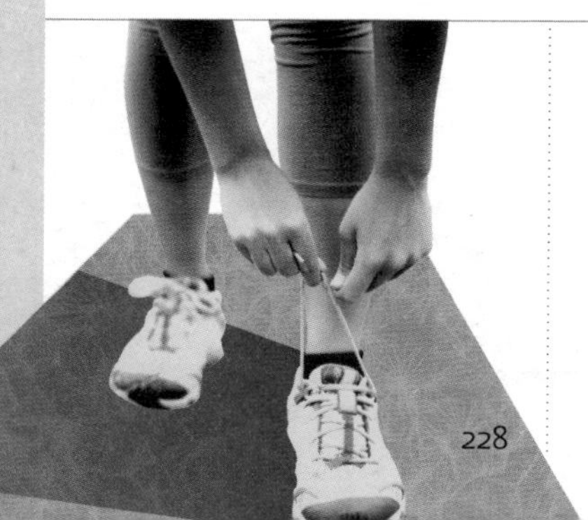

Find Healthy Ways to Relieve Stress

Always be on the lookout for ways to reduce your stress levels, and include stress relief in your daily schedule.

Find running or walking partners, join intramural sports teams, take yoga classes, go on outdoor club trips, participate in theater productions, play in a band, and so on. Make a list of things that work for you. Keep this list handy so that you can practice effective stress relief at a moment's notice, especially during exam periods.

Act PLAN MY PRIORITIES a.m. p.m.

23 monday

24 tuesday

25 wednesday

26 thursday

27 friday

28 saturday Vesak

29 sunday

Check REVIEW & REFLECT ✓ Did I achieve my weekly goals? → What didn't get accomplished?

Use Counseling Services

College adjustment and related academic and social challenges may necessitate extra support for emotional and mental well-being during the college years.

Using the services of your college counseling office can be an important support in making sure you are emotionally well and healthy to handle these challenges.

* ***Find out what services are offered, how to access the services, insurance and payment issues, special programs offered such as group counseling and individual counseling.***
* ***Complete any necessary registration paperwork at the beginning of the semester so that you are able to immediately use the counseling support services.***

Know the signs of depression, anxiety, stress, trauma, and so on and get help and assistance immediately if needed.

* ***Ask to see a counselor with experience in your area of need.***
* ***Be specific, if possible, with the challenges and issues you are facing.***
* ***Write down questions you want to ask the counselor or physician working with you.***
* ***If you have a physical or an emotional health issue, immediately seek assistance.***
* ***If you have problems and issues caused by alcohol or drugs, do not delay getting help.***

Get help at the first sign of difficulty—make good use of the counseling services.

Record IMPORTANT EVENTS

sunday	monday
6	7
13 Mother's Day	14
20	21
27	28 Memorial Day

Act Can't get it all done? Prioritize!

MAY 2012

tuesday	wednesday	thursday	friday	saturday
1	2	3	4	5
8	9	10	11	12
15	16	17	18	19
22	23	24	25	26
29	30	31		

✓ **Check** Did you finish your important tasks and goals?

Think THIS WEEK'S GOALS, PROJECTS, IDEAS

Record ASSIGNMENTS & TESTS

Seek Leadership Opportunities

Actively seek leadership positions early in your college career.

Join organizations and seek out ways to be actively involved. Volunteer for responsibilities that will help you prepare for future leadership roles. It is important to prepare yourself for potential leadership in your chosen profession. If your school offers formal leadership development programs, consider enrolling in them.

Act PLAN MY PRIORITIES

a.m. p.m.

30 APR monday

1 tuesday

2 wednesday

3 thursday

4 friday

5 saturday

6 sunday

Check REVIEW & REFLECT

✓ Did I achieve my weekly goals? → What didn't get accomplished?

Think THIS WEEK'S GOALS, PROJECTS, IDEAS

Record ASSIGNMENTS & TESTS

Use the Counseling Services

Use the school's counseling services; their support will be valuable when you hit rough times.

Find out what services are offered, how to access them, and how to submit insurance claims. Investigate special programs such as group counseling and individual counseling. Complete registration paperwork at the beginning of the term, so that you will be able to use the services immediately in a crisis, and keep contact information available.

Act PLAN MY PRIORITIES

a.m.

p.m.

7 monday

8 tuesday

9 wednesday

10 thursday

11 friday

12 saturday

13 sunday

Mother's Day

Check REVIEW & REFLECT

✓ Did I achieve my weekly goals? → What didn't get accomplished?

Think THIS WEEK'S GOALS, PROJECTS, IDEAS

Record ASSIGNMENTS & TESTS

Use Career Services

Use college or university career services; they are an important resource.

Investigate the services your campus career office offers, and stay connected with the office throughout your college years. If possible, schedule meetings with companies that come to campus to interview students for potential employment. This will help you learn what employers value in a college graduate. Bring a professional, current résumé to each interview, and dress for success. Be well-rested, alert, and engaged in the interview process. Research the company and come with a list of questions for the interviewer, but don't ask for information that is available on the company's website.

Act PLAN MY PRIORITIES

a.m. p.m.

14 monday

15 tuesday

16 wednesday

17 thursday

18 friday

19 saturday

20 sunday

Check REVIEW & REFLECT ✓ Did I achieve my weekly goals? → What didn't get accomplished?

Think THIS WEEK'S GOALS, PROJECTS, IDEAS

Record ASSIGNMENTS & TESTS

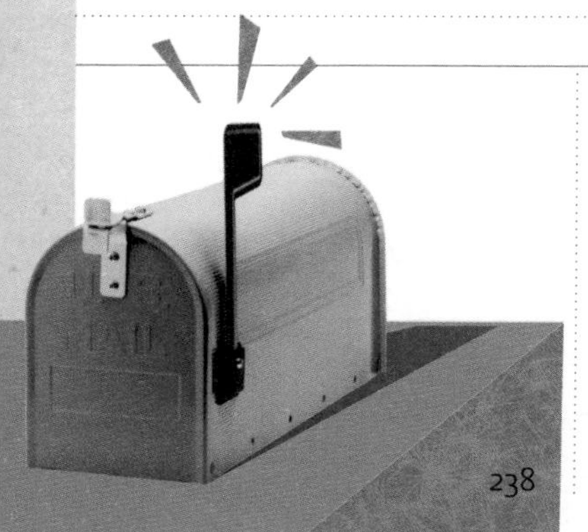

Request Reference Letters

Request letters of reference well in advance of applications for internships, graduate programs, fellowships and scholarships, or jobs.

Carefully select faculty and others who know you very well to write references for you. Provide them with clear information and with stamped, addressed envelopes. Offer to list things about yourself that the recommender might find useful. Follow up with an e-mail reminder before the due date. Don't forget to thank the recommenders with personal notes, and let them know when their recommendations contribute to your success.

Act PLAN MY PRIORITIES a.m. p.m.

21 monday

22 tuesday

23 wednesday

24 thursday

25 friday

26 saturday

27 sunday

Check REVIEW & REFLECT ✓ Did I achieve my weekly goals? → What didn't get accomplished?

Think THIS WEEK'S GOALS, PROJECTS, IDEAS

Record ASSIGNMENTS & TESTS

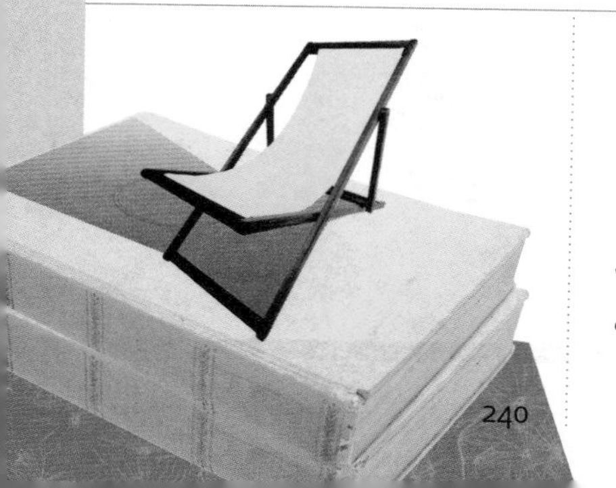

Make Summers Count

Make certain that your summers enhance your academic and career goals.

Carefully plan how you will use your breaks from campus. Look for work or other experiences that will connect your summer activities to your academic studies and career goals. If an experience is positive, ask your supervisor for a letter of reference. Write about what you are learning from both positive and negative experiences, and discuss challenging situations with those who are more experienced than you.

Act PLAN MY PRIORITIES a.m. p.m.

28 MAY monday Memorial Day

29 MAY tuesday

30 MAY wednesday

31 MAY thursday

1 friday

2 saturday

3 sunday

Check REVIEW & REFLECT ✓ Did I achieve my weekly goals? → What didn't get accomplished?

Maintain a Portfolio of your Work

Portfolios that document your academic progress are very helpful for present and future applications.

- ***Develop, maintain, and constantly update a portfolio of representative, high-quality work for each course taken.***
- ***Keep this file electronically and in hard copy.***
- ***Reflect upon and review this material regularly; use this process to improve your writing, presentation skills, and so on.***
- ***Keeping a portfolio of your best work can be helpful in numerous ways, such as documentation when applying for scholarships, internships, job interviews, and so on.***

Gathering and reflecting upon your work is important for seeing and documenting progress in your studies. Reflection is also important and helpful for enhancing and improving the quality of your work.

- ***Ask students who are excelling in their college work to identify helpful tips and hints, including how they improve their work products.***
- ***Early in your college career, organize a system that works well for you to identify and keep work that is of outstanding quality.***
- ***Collect work from a variety of courses and across disciplines.***
- ***Jot down ways you might use your portfolio information in the future.***
- ***Be creative; be strategic about using this material to improve your work products.***
- ***Ask trusted peers and professors to review and critique your best work—with the intent of improvement.***

Record IMPORTANT EVENTS

sunday	monday
3	4
10	11
17 Father's Day	18
24	25

Act Can't get it all done? Prioritize!

JUNE 2012

tuesday	wednesday	thursday	friday	saturday
			1	2
5	6	7	8	9
12	13	14	15	16
19	20	21	22	23
26	27	28	29	30

Check Did you finish your important tasks and goals?

Think THIS WEEK'S GOALS, PROJECTS, IDEAS

Record ASSIGNMENTS & TESTS

Do Internships

Do internships, whether paid or voluntary.

Such internships are a valuable way to apply your academic knowledge to the real world of work. Early in your college career, investigate appropriate internships, and work to develop the prerequisites for these internships. If possible, talk with students who have been placed with organizations you are interested in. Find out what was positive about the internship and what areas could have been improved. Try to anticipate areas of difficulty and be proactive in your planning for an optimal internship.

Act PLAN MY PRIORITIES

a.m. ✓→

p.m. ✓→

4 monday

5 tuesday

6 wednesday

7 thursday

8 friday

9 saturday

10 sunday

Check REVIEW & REFLECT

✓ Did I achieve my weekly goals? → What didn't get accomplished?

Think THIS WEEK'S GOALS, PROJECTS, IDEAS

Record ASSIGNMENTS & TESTS

Access Alumni Networks

Access and learn about potential connections with alumni and related networks and services.

Such contacts can be your best resources as you enter your career field. For example, volunteering for alumni events can put you in touch with many seasoned professionals in your field or geographic area. Talk with alumni working in jobs that interest you, and ask to be notified when potential internships or similar opportunities arise.

Act PLAN MY PRIORITIES a.m. p.m.

11 monday

12 tuesday

13 wednesday

14 thursday

15 friday

16 saturday

17 sunday Father's Day

Check REVIEW & REFLECT ✓ Did I achieve my weekly goals? → What didn't get accomplished?

Think THIS WEEK'S GOALS, PROJECTS, IDEAS

Record ASSIGNMENTS & TESTS

Write Thank You Letters

Write personal letters of thanks and appreciation.

A handwritten note always shows good manners and an appropriate attitude; a prompt e-mail will do in a pinch. Any personal assistance (such as a letter of recommendation or extraordinary attention and support) from faculty, staff, or advisors should be gratefully acknowledged. Several people a month may merit your thanks, so be sure to keep a supply of note cards on hand.

Act PLAN MY PRIORITIES a.m. p.m.

18 monday

19 tuesday

20 wednesday

21 thursday

22 friday

23 saturday

24 sunday

Check REVIEW & REFLECT ✓ Did I achieve my weekly goals? → What didn't get accomplished?

Think THIS WEEK'S GOALS, PROJECTS, IDEAS

Record ASSIGNMENTS & TESTS

Maintain a Portfolio of Your Work

Develop, maintain, and constantly update a portfolio of representative high-quality work for each course you take.

Keep this file electronically and in hard copy. Reflect upon and review this material regularly as you strive to improve your writing and presentation skills. The portfolio will be useful as documentation for job and scholarship applications.

Act PLAN MY PRIORITIES

a.m. p.m.

25 monday

26 tuesday

27 wednesday

28 thursday

29 friday

30 saturday

1 JULY sunday

Check REVIEW & REFLECT ✓ Did I achieve my weekly goals? → What didn't get accomplished?

Record IMPORTANT EVENTS

sunday	monday
1	2
8	9
15	16
22	23
29	30

Improve Written Communication Skills

Regardless of your career path, you need to have good written communication skills along with good public speaking skills.

Writing is typically required across the college curriculum, and it is a critically important skill for your college success as well as post college life.

* ***Practice written communication skills daily and request feedback on how you can improve.***
* ***Work ahead, editing and rereading your work numerous times prior to submission.***
* ***Constantly work to improve your writing.***

Many colleges and universities have a writing center to assist students in becoming better writers.

* ***Find out where the center is located and use it frequently.***
* ***Learn if the writing center accepts electronic submissions and how much lead time is needed for feedback.***
* ***Take advantage of training sessions and seminars they conduct to assist students in becoming stronger writers and communicators.***
* ***Use the writing center for major written assignments, no matter how good of a writer you think you are—you can always improve your written communication skills.***

Your writing is sometimes the first and only introduction of you and your abilities. For example, a written job or scholarship application is the first indication of your abilities. Work hard to showcase your best writing; ask for ways to improve your writing from professionals and capable peers.

Act Can't get it all done? Prioritize!

JULY 2012

tuesday	wednesday	thursday	friday	saturday
3	4 Independence Day	5	6	7
10	11	12	13	14
17	18	19	20 Ramadan	21
24	25	26	27	28
31				

Check Did you finish your important tasks and goals?

Think THIS WEEK'S GOALS, PROJECTS, IDEAS

Record ASSIGNMENTS & TESTS

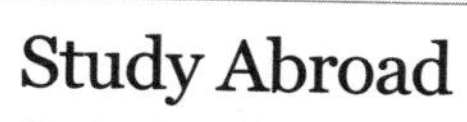

Study Abroad

Study abroad during your undergraduate years.

Develop a four-year strategic approach to your college or university experience, and plan carefully for each year. It is critically important to develop global views and perspectives as part of your college experience. Find out where your school has agreements for study-abroad programs, and be sure the credits you earn abroad will count toward your graduation.

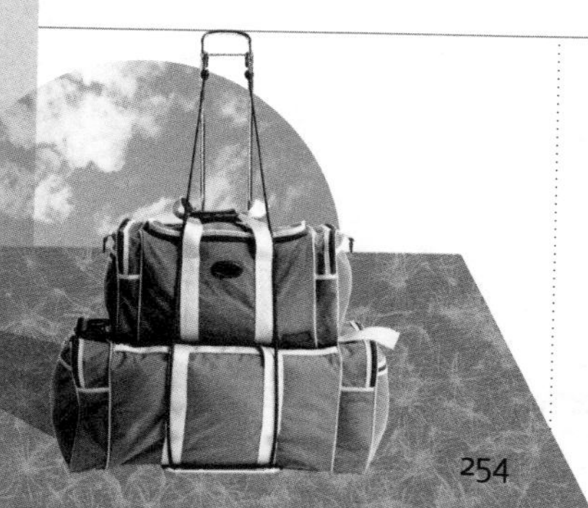

Act PLAN MY PRIORITIES

a.m. p.m.

2 monday

3 tuesday

4 wednesday

Independence Day

5 thursday

6 friday

7 saturday

8 sunday

Check REVIEW & REFLECT ✓ Did I achieve my weekly goals? → What didn't get accomplished?

Think THIS WEEK'S GOALS, PROJECTS, IDEAS

Record ASSIGNMENTS & TESTS

Improve Written Communication Skills

They are critical to your success now and in the future.

Practice daily and request feedback on your work. Find out if your school has a writing center and use it for help on every major assignment. Learn how and when to submit work, and plan for the stated response time. If the center offers formal training, use it. No matter how strong your writing is, you can improve.

Act PLAN MY PRIORITIES

a.m.

p.m.

9 monday

10 tuesday

11 wednesday

12 thursday

13 friday

14 saturday

15 sunday

Check REVIEW & REFLECT ✓ Did I achieve my weekly goals? → What didn't get accomplished?

Think THIS WEEK'S GOALS, PROJECTS, IDEAS

Record ASSIGNMENTS & TESTS

Your Tip!

Reflect on the past year and the 50 Tips for College Success.

What worked well for you? Write down any additional tips you've discovered during your first year at college. What advice do you have for others beginning their college journey?

Act PLAN MY PRIORITIES

a.m. p.m.

16 monday

17 tuesday

18 wednesday

19 thursday

20 friday

Ramadan

21 saturday

22 sunday

Check REVIEW & REFLECT

✓ Did I achieve my weekly goals? → What didn't get accomplished?

Think THIS WEEK'S GOALS, PROJECTS, IDEAS

Record ASSIGNMENTS & TESTS

The Internet: Your Personal Sidekick

The Internet is well-known for creating a disappearing act of your free time, but it can actually save you time and money! Check out these helpful—and free—websites.

- Time Management: www.google.com/calendar
- Money Management: www.mint.com
- Federal Tuition Assistance: www.fafsa.ed.gov
- Scholarships: www.fastweb.com
- Nutrition Management: www.thedailyplate.com

Act PLAN MY PRIORITIES a.m. p.m.

23 monday

24 tuesday

25 wednesday

26 thursday

27 friday

28 saturday

29 sunday

Check REVIEW & REFLECT ✓ Did I achieve my weekly goals? → What didn't get accomplished?

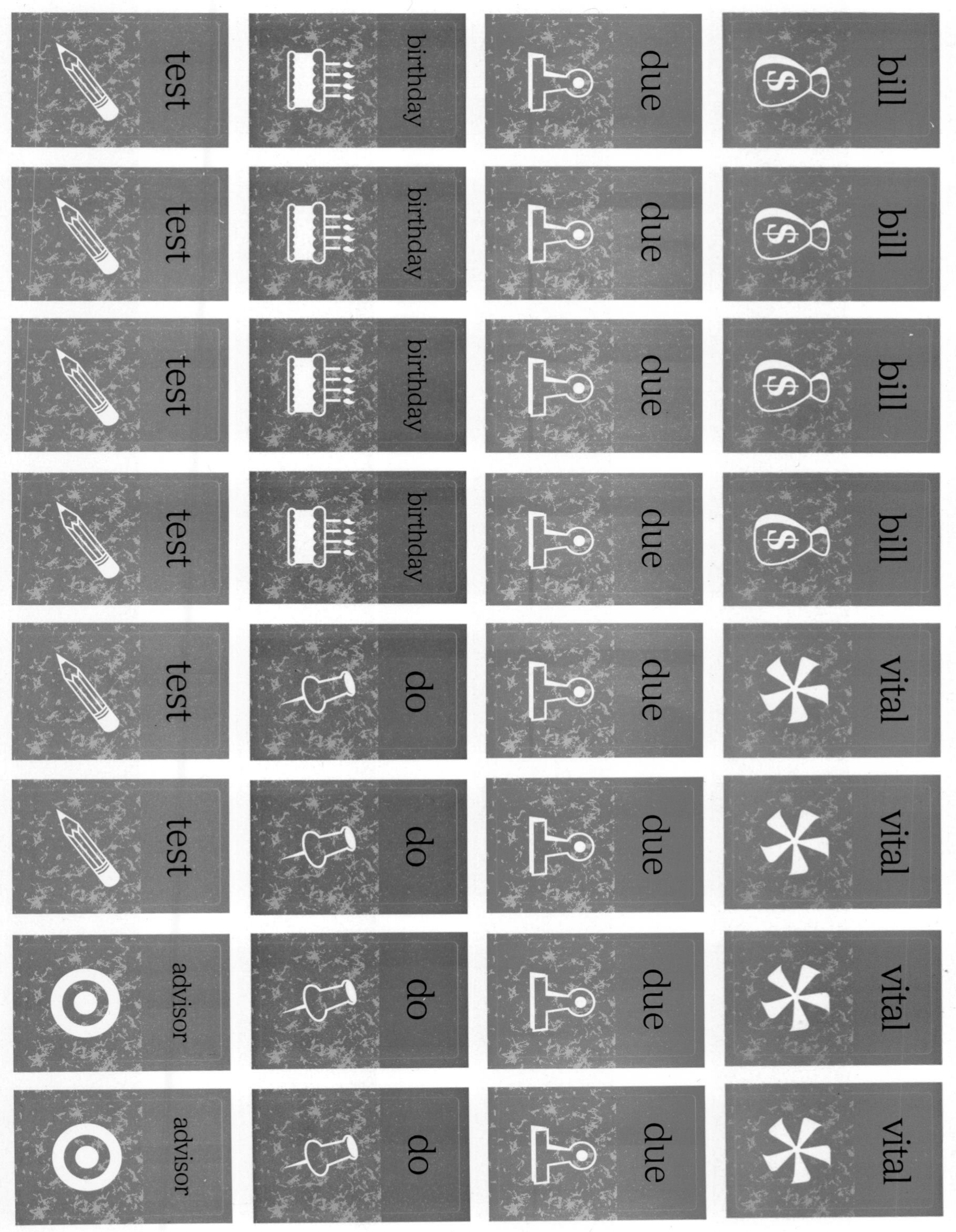

Use these stickies to help you **find important things** quickly.